TO CATCH A TROUT

TO CATCH A TROUT

A Complete Fly Fishing Guide
for Beginners

NICK MASKREY

*With a Foreword by
Sir Michael Hordern, CBE*

SOUVENIR PRESS

First published 1991 by Souvenir Press Ltd,
43 Great Russell Street, London WC1B 3PA
and simultaneously in Canada

ISBN 0 285 63026 1

Printed and bound in Great Britain by
WBC Ltd, Bridgend

Photoset by Rowland Phototypesetting Ltd
Bury St Edmunds, Suffolk

To Lesley

who came fishing once but discovered nettles and mosquitoes.
She has never since objected when I have fished without her.

And when the timorous Trout I wait
to take, and he devours my bait,
How poor thing, sometimes I find,
Will captivate a greedy mind:
And when none bite, I praise the wise
Whom vain allurements ne'er surprise.

Piscato 's song, *The Compleat Angler*
Izaak Walton

Foreword

by
Sir Michael Hordern, CBE

This coming trout season I shall stop and *think*. Ever since I caught my first fish when I was five years old I have dashed up the bank for the next one. Describing such-like fishermen, Mr Maskrey writes: 'If only they could be happy to stay beside the river and see the fish they catch as a bonus for just being there.' Wise words.

I shall slow down this coming spring on Usk and Itchen. Armed with the experienced wisdom in these pages, I shall fish finer points, I will not tie, nor will I carry, too many patterns of fly (though those I do carry will have benefited from the uncomplicated dressings in Chapter 6) and I will absorb the author's excellent observations on the trout's vision.

This book is sub-titled 'A Complete Fly Fishing Guide for Beginners'; it is certainly that and much more than that, and becomes, without being heavy, progressively more instructive chapter by chapter. I wish I had had sight of it seventy years ago!

Contents

Preface

It was my original intention to give a description of the remarkable beauty of the southern English water meadows. I wanted to convey the buzz of anticipation I feel every time I see a trout rise to a fly that struggles on the surface of the crystal world that is the chalk stream. In the end I decided that these are pleasures the reader can enjoy and see for himself. No words I write can express the beauty of the trout or its surroundings, nor can I explain why, after 27 years of dry fly fishing, I am still utterly absorbed by it.

My only impatience with the subject comes from the snobbish mystique which seems to have grown up over such a humble sport. Perhaps it is because its popularity has meant that the southern chalk streams are usually expensive to fish and therefore enjoy a certain exclusivity. The purpose of this book is to do away with the myth of dry fly fishing and to put in its place a sensible approach that will help in the relatively simple process of catching trout with a nymph or floating fly.

My choice has been to begin at the beginning, so I must apologise in advance to the experienced fisherman who may find the first chapter a statement of the obvious—but when I started fly fishing I could not find a book on the dry fly that assumed I knew nothing, and as a result it took me longer than it should have done to find out the first principles.

No beginner wants to have to read straight through a book which gives him a snowstorm of facts that only serve to confuse. I have therefore tried to give enough information in the first chapter to enable a complete beginner to read that one chapter and then go fishing. Once he has sampled the delights of the dry fly he will be keen to learn more and may then want to read on.

The book is based on my own day-to-day fly fishing experience, on observations made during my fishing outings, and is not intended to be a gospel. It is simply one person's view giving details of the methods I have evolved to overcome problems that have been presented to me. There are few cast-iron rules in fly fishing. Frequently there may be several solutions to a single fishing problem, and what may work on one day may well be a disaster on the next. The details and experiences I give are descriptions of the way I have sometimes managed to overcome a few of the problems.

I am no academic, so there will be no erudite arguments. I have simply discovered that the common fisherman's most valuable asset is observation. If I have read something that seemed to be sensible, but my own observation has shown it to be untrue, then I have rejected it. I hope that the reader will adopt the same attitude to this book.

In a number of places throughout the text I have referred to 'fishermen' or have used the male pronoun. I have no wish to insult the many women who go fishing, but to refer to 'fisherwomen' or 'fisherperson' is obviously clumsy and incongruous, so I trust female readers will forgive my apparent male chauvinism, which is used only for expedience.

I should like to thank my good friend Bob Schröder for reading this book as it was being written and for his valuable observations which frequently led to some amusing arguments. I should also like to thank my wife Lesley, whose spelling and grammar are better than mine, and who took the trouble to read many thousands of words on a subject which has bored her for at least 26 years. Thanks, too, to Graham Mole whose idea for a fishing book gave me an introduction to the publishers, and to Taff Price who generously allowed me to use his excellent photographs of natural flies. The pictures of artificial flies were taken by the superb photographer Peter Gathercole. My thanks to John Goddard who came to my rescue with a photograph of the natural medium olive dun, and to Dave Tait for his pictures of the natural iron blue dun and blue winged olive dun.

Some of the material used in this book was originally published in *Trout and Salmon*, *Salmon, Trout and Seatrout*, *Countrysport* and *Practical Gamefishing* magazines.

Nick Maskrey
Blandford
Dorset.

Chapter One

The lane that ran down to the fishing at the New Forest farm also formed part of a stream bed. As I walked from my car to the bottom of the hill I could look into the crystal-clear water and see insect larvae going about their business. This was my first insight into aquatic insect life and was to be the start of a learning process that continues to this day.

From the time when I was first taught to cast a fly by my wife's godmother's family, at the age of 20, I read all that I could find about fly fishing. My first fly rod was a converted spinning rod. I changed the rings on it and made a longer top section which I took from an old coarse fishing split cane rod that I had.

Initially I bought day tickets from pubs in the Hampshire Avon valley and cut my teeth with the dry fly by fishing for dace. The lightning strike necessary to hook a dace was to be my downfall for some time after I started trout fishing.

Fishing for dace helped to improve my casting, and when I moved house to West Surrey I was fortunate to meet a local farmer with some trout fishing on the upper waters of the River Wey. His invitation to me was to give me my first real taste of fishing for trout with a dry fly. On that memorable first evening I saw the water boil with rising fish. I had no idea what flies these fish were taking, and after spending some time casting all over the river I eventually hooked and landed my first decent-sized trout on the dry fly. Several others had taken my fly before this, but try as I might I could not hook them, although I felt the weight of several of them before they came off. The one I caught had hooked itself.

During a conversation with my local tackle dealer following that first experience, he told me that I was striking too quickly. It was important, he said, to wait for the trout's head to go down after it had taken the fly. 'Repeat to yourself, "Got you, you devil", before trying to set the hook,' he told me. Then, he said, the hook should be set in the trout's jaw by a gentle flick of the wrist. Catching trout was not like fishing for dace, he advised. I was anxious to put his advice to the test and wangled myself another invitation on the River Wey.

The man in the tackle shop also sold me some flies which he had tied himself. Among these were some sedge flies which he recommended I use in the evening. He had deduced from my description that the rising fish I had seen on the evening of my previous visit were almost certainly feeding on sedges.

Armed with my new knowledge and the flies, I returned to the river. I saw very few fish rise all day, and because of my inexperience it took a long time to put my fly over a rising fish satisfactorily, even when I did find one. When I eventually managed this, more by luck than judgement, up came the trout. Despite my excitement, I remembered the magic phrase and, wonder of wonders, there was a struggling trout on the end of my line. I caught four fish that day and as a result I believed I was an expert.

Shortly after this I was fortunate enough to meet the bailiff of a local still-water trout fishery. He invited me for a day at his lakes. The fishing there was predominantly with wet flies. He laughed out loud when he saw my rod and lent me a good rod, reel and line. When he saw my casting he tutted! He gave me a crash course in casting and took me out in a boat on one of the three lakes in his charge.

We were to become good friends. He showed me how he made his own flies, and through his generosity I had many days' fishing on water that the members were paying a fortune to fish. Although all forms of fishing have always fascinated me, my very early experiences on the River Wey, and before that on the Hampshire Avon and Welsh rivers, had taught me that dry fly fishing was what I really wanted to do. I love rivers, and the excitement of seeing fish in the water, apparently waiting to be caught, is irresistible.

My bailiff friend had formerly been a keeper on Dorset's River Frome, and as a result knew a great deal about dry fly fishing. He advised on flies to buy and he also sold me a decent cane rod, a Kingfisher silk line, and suggested a reel that would suit me.

I took to making trips to the River Usk at Brecon and fishing the dry fly on the cheap club waters there. I caught many small trout, but nothing of any size. The real turning point came when one day I saw an advertisement inserted by Ringwood Anglers' Club, offering fishing for trout on the Hampshire Avon and the rivers Test and Itchen. The subscription then, I believe, was just £10 a year. At last, here seemed the opportunity to fish the classic chalk streams I had read so much about but thought were wildly beyond my financial reach.

In due course my membership card arrived, and with it a booklet listing all the available water. I looked up the beats of the Test and Itchen and established where the fishing on the Avon was. The booklet carried maps of all the water, with detailed descriptions of how to get there. One of the waters was the farm in the New Forest which I mentioned at the beginning of this chapter.

I must dwell on this place because for me it crystallised all the magic of dry fly fishing. The stream at the bottom of the hill was one of the smaller carriers of the mighty River Avon, and most of the remaining trout fishing on the farm was made up of other carriers which were originally designed to flood the water meadows each spring.

An explanation of the old system of irrigating and fertilising land would be useful to anyone who plans to fish the southern chalk streams. Very little of the original pattern of these streams and rivers remains today. The hand of man has been at work on their routes to the sea since earliest times. The Test and Itchen, in particular, hardly existed as flowing streams at all. They were simply a string of marshes that filled the lower ground and were connected together by a myriad of small rivulets and brooks.

In order to drain the marshes, so that this very fertile land could be used for agriculture, the streams connecting the marshes were widened and deepened and ditches were dug so that they carried the water from the sodden land into the main-stream channel. After a few years, however, the fertility of the drained land began to decrease, so a way had to be found of replenishing the meadows, to spread the rich silt from the main stream back on to the land. This was achieved by the construction of a series of sluices that could be opened and closed, allowing the water level on any given area to be raised or lowered.

Although modern fertilisers have made the old system redundant, many of the original sluices and watercourses on the chalk streams have been retained so that flow levels can be adjusted and accidental flooding avoided. This has been a huge blessing for the fly fisher because it means that the evenness of flow of the rivers and the carriers has been preserved. Because the rivers are spring fed and subject to detailed control, they keep much the same level throughout the year. The original carriers and drains have produced many small streams crossing and recrossing beautiful southern farmland, and they all provide a home and breeding place for trout.

This system had been used extensively on the New Forest farm, with the result that there were three main carriers and their drains, as well as the main river, all providing fascinating fishing. Every sluice pool held many fish and each seemed to have its resident giant.

The trout that inhabit these rivers and carriers live largely on the insect life that is indigenous to them. It is not necessary to have a vast knowledge of insect life in order to be a competent trout fisher, but some knowledge does help. When I first started trout fishing I did not even realise that the artificial flies I had been advised to use where imitations of flies which bred in the water, but as I read more and spent more time by the river I gradually built up a knowledge of water fly life.

Before my very early experience on the River Wey taught me that I had to present the trout with an imitation of a fly that was floating on the water, I had not noticed these flies on the water or in the air, nor had I questioned where they came from. I suppose I thought they were land-bred insects or were something like mosquitoes or house flies which happened to alight on the surface of the river. Gradually a picture of what really took place dawned upon me.

The whole art of fishing the dry fly is based on attempting to imitate the appearance of a natural fly on the water.

It must be explained that in every reasonably clean river and stream in the country there is insect life that is dependent upon it. These insects inhabit the silt and gravel bottom of the stream and the plants that grow in it. They are the swimming larvae of various flies and are known to the fisherman as 'nymphs'. The nymphs will eventually hatch on the surface of the water as recognisable winged insects.

They are of interest to trout in three stages of their life-cycle. The first is the sub-surface nymph; the second is the 'dun', a recognisable fly which has hatched from the nymph stage; and the third is the 'spinner', a fully formed fly that is in mating livery and capable of reproducing its species.

Below the surface of every area of water there are nymphs zooming about feeding, either on other living creatures, or on algae or other organic matter in the water. These nymphs have hatched from eggs laid by the parent flies.

Eventually the nymphs, usually after one year, decide it is time to ascend, normally inert, to the surface of the water. They transpose within the surface film into a winged insect—not unlike a large mosquito in appearance. It is at this stage that the untutored eye first has a chance to witness exactly what a water fly looks like. It is a minute sailing boat, floating on the water with its wings held aloft, tail curling behind and legs spread wide on the surface tension to give it stability.

In this state the fly is consumed avidly by fish, waterfowl and birds. It is probably at its most vulnerable and in any one hatching period thousands will die in the jaws of predators. Those that escape take off from the surface and flutter clumsily to the nearest bankside vegetation, where they rest. Here, in the privacy of the undergrowth, they undergo another transformation. From drab little creatures they become brightly coloured and their wings sparkle with translucence.

These perfect flies are known to entomologists as 'imagos' and are now in their mating livery. On warm evenings they can be seen dancing over bankside vegetation, rising and falling in effortless flight—apparently delighting in their aerial dexterity after their awkward movement in the dun stage of development.

Having joined with the males in their evening dance, the females return to the water to lay their eggs. Some dip to the surface and, with each fleeting contact, discharge many eggs through the surface film, which drift to the weed, mud and stones on the bottom. Others climb down reeds, bridge supports or even wading anglers' boots, to discharge their eggs under water. Here the eggs remain inert until they hatch into nymphs and the whole life-cycle begins again. The exhausted parent flies fall, in their death throes, to the surface of the water and the fish feed on the corpses. The flies in this stage are called 'spent spinners' by the fisherman.

This life-cycle applies to the species of fly that are most important to the dry fly fisher, the order Ephemeridae (originally a Greek word which means lasting only one day). There are several other flies which are also important, but more of those later.

The next step is to examine the trout's relationship with the fly. It must be remembered that flies are not necessarily the trout's main source of food, but they concern the fisherman most of all, simply because they offer the best chance of catching the fish.

On southern chalk streams in particular, there are written rules which are designed to make fishing more difficult and therefore more absorbing. On most, only a fly may be fished and it may only be fished upstream—that is, cast upstream of the fisherman and allowed to float down towards him with no drag on the line induced by him.

Many chalk stream clubs and syndicates do allow the fishing of a sunken fly, but this must also be cast upstream and is normally tied to imitate a nymph. Whatever your opinion of the rule about fishing upstream, it is applied universally on southern chalk streams (and many others) and it is therefore necessary to master this technique.

As I have explained, of the four basic stages of fly life—egg, nymph, dun and spinner—the trout is interested in the last three as a source of food. It will consume flies in all three stages of development, sometimes feeding exclusively on just one stage at a time, but at others feeding on all three if they happen to be available simultaneously.

It is argued that more flies are consumed by trout at the nymphal stage than at any other time. This is probably true, but unless we don mask and snorkel there is only one simple way we can establish what the fish is eating. That is by catching it and examining its stomach contents—but it can be difficult to catch the fish if you do not know what it is eating!

Fortunately most dry fly running water is clear, and so observation becomes essential. The first rule is that when you spot a fish, either by seeing it in the water or by noticing some disturbance it may make on the surface, it is important to take time to study what is going on. See if you can spot in what stage flies are being consumed. If they are being taken as nymphs you will see the fish move from side to side under water, usually with small darting movements. If the water is clear enough you may even be able to see the trout's mouth open and close.

Because the trout is an efficient feeding machine, it will normally find the best possible place in the river to intercept food, and will remain there until it becomes inhospitable. This is fortunate for the fisherman. When he gets to know a particular water he will know where the fish normally lie. It must, however, be remembered that a fish will not normally expend more energy on catching a fly than he will gain from eating it. This means that your casting of the artificial fly must be accurate.

The best position for placing your fly is roughly two feet upstream of the trout's rising position. This is further complicated by the pattern of currents bringing the natural fly to the fish. It is easy if the current is approaching the fish's nose head-on—but this is rarely the case. Although the fish may be lying with his head directly upstream, his food can be carried towards him by several routes. These are determined by the pattern the water makes around objects protruding from the stream bed, or by overhanging branches and other interruptions in the general current, so the fly must be cast into a position where it will naturally be carried over the fish.

Even on a water you have never fished before it is not difficult to spot likely places where the fish lie in wait for their quarry. Because they must expend as little energy as possible on feeding, it is important that they find a place that requires as little effort as possible to remain stationary. Thus they will lie in front of a weed plant or stone, where the build-up of water against the object forms a pressure wave that will hold the trout head-on to the current, with just a gentle wag of his tail and twitch of his pectoral fins to keep him in balance and hold his position.

From this vantage point his upwardly-biased vision will warn him of any insect approaching on or below the surface. All he has to do is raise or lower his head, or turn from side to side, in order to intercept his quarry.

Stand on a bridge over any chalk stream and, with a pair of polarising glasses, search the water for fish lying below you. Pick on one fish and watch his actions. So much can be learned just by looking.

When I arrived at the New Forest farm for the first time, armed with fishing rod, line, reel and flies, I had already come some way in learning the fishing process. By this time, thanks to my bailiff friend, I had learned that it was vital to have balanced tackle. It is most important that the line should be the right weight to make the rod 'work' properly, for if it is of insufficient weight the rod will not act like a spring to propel the line out across the water when casting. If it is too heavy, the line will strain the rod and make its action 'soggy'. All good rods have a recommended line weight printed on them. This is indicated either by the letters AFTM followed by a number (which indicates the line weight) or by the symbol # and a number.

I believe that it is impossible to learn casting from a book. My advice is to buy a fly fishing magazine and find an advertisement for a casting school near you where you can get lessons. Learning to cast properly is vital and it is worth spending a little money on this part of fly fishing.

Probably the most suitable length of rod for general dry fly fishing is eight feet six inches. Fly lines are coded to give an indication of their weight, whether they float or sink and what their configuration is. For example, take a line that is marked DT6F. DT stands for a double tapered configuration. This means that the line is fattest in the centre and tapers towards each end, giving more weight to 'work' the rod as the line is extended while casting. The number 6 denotes the weight of the line and F stands for 'floating'. There are various configurations and weights of line, but a double-tapered floater is by far the most commonly used for dry fly fishing on rivers. It has the advantage of being able to be reversed on the reel when the leading end of the taper becomes worn.

Also of importance is the right length of leader or trace (the length of nylon which is attached to the fly line and to which the fly is knotted). The leader should be roughly the same length as the rod and, like the fly line, it is tapered and the thickest end fastened to the fly line. Proprietary tapered casts can be bought in various thicknesses. These are given an 'X' rating, which refers to the diameter of the leader at its thinnest part, namely the point to which the fly is attached. Bearing in mind the size of the fly you are using and the estimated weight of the fish you are likely to catch, it is important that you use the finest point possible.

Four or five 'X' are probably the most useful sizes for general dry fly fishing. Remember that the lower the X number is, the thicker the point will be, so a 3X point is thicker and therefore stronger than, for example, 5X. While there may be virtue in strength, thicker leaders are more easily detectable by the trout and this is why you should fish as fine as possible.

For the beginner, the quality of the reel is probably not so important. So long as it is reasonably light and sturdy, has a smooth running action and will hold 30 yards of double-tapered line plus a reasonable length of backing line beneath it, almost any fly reel on the market will do. Later, when you become more experienced and have the opportunity to try other people's tackle, you will decide which reel suits your needs best.

Special backing line can be bought to put on the reel before the fly line. It serves two purposes. First, it provides a safety margin in case the full length of the fly line (normally 30 yards) is pulled off the reel by a charging fish; and second, it allows the fly line to be wound on the reel in a wider arc so that it is not damaged by tight compression and has less tendency to coil while in use off the reel (sometimes called 'line memory'). Another advantage is that the line is closer to the reel rim, effectively allowing a faster rate of recovery back onto the reel when rewinding.

You will also need a bottle of good fly oil (I find Permaflote the best) and a folding landing net that can be clipped on your belt. When buying a landing net, I advise getting one that folds with a hinge between the telescopic handle and the fixed frame. Some nets have collapsible frames and they can be very difficult to erect if they become tangled with the net. The last thing you want is to be fighting a fish with one hand and your net with the other!

On many waters a pair of thigh waders is essential. I always wear mine. Advice on tackle is probably best obtained from your casting teacher, but much of your choice will probably be dictated by price and any experienced tackle dealer will tell you the best buy. I would advise you to buy the best rod you can possibly afford and not to cut costs on fly lines. My personal favourite is Air-cel Supreme, but I know many good and experienced fishermen who swear by Cortland lines. Both Hardy and Orvis lines also have excellent reputations.

You need a box for your artificial flies. There are plenty of inexpensive plastic boxes on the market, which have separate sections for the different patterns of fly. The best boxes should have separate lids for each compartment, so that in breezy weather you do not risk losing all your flies, blown out of the box by a sudden gust.

Also needed is a pair of small scissors. A useful pattern is made by Hardy Bros. These have scissor-type serrated blades, but with a flat area on the end of each blade which is useful for gripping and removing the hook from a fish which has been hooked in the back of its mouth. You will also need something on which to dry your flies. A piece of kitchen roll will do, but I find that the best and most absorbent device is a piece cut from the head of a Vileda Super Mop. This material is like very thin sponge. The fly can be squeezed between the layers of sponge before re-oiling. It is important that most dry flies float very well, so it is necessary to dry and re-oil them at regular intervals. Fish slime on a fly (when you have been lucky enough to catch a trout) should be washed off in the stream and the fly dried and re-oiled.

When dry fly fishing, a pair of polarising glasses is a great advantage. These help you to see through the surface reflections on the water, making spotting fish and studying the bottom of the stream much easier. Be sure that the lenses really are the polarising type. A simple test in a shop is to take another pair the same as those you are planning to buy and, while wearing one pair, rotate the other radially in front of them. As the lenses are rotated you will see that they appear to go black as the light fails to pass through the two planes. One piece of advice: buy glasses with lenses of the lightest possible tint, so that when you are beside the river you will be able to see your own and natural flies easily while fishing.

If you intend to kill some of the fish you catch you will also need a 'priest', which is a small club for killing fish humanely. It is vital that the fish should suffer as little as possible when being dispatched, so you need something that will give a sharp single blow to the top of its head, killing it instantly.

Finally, a marrow scoop is useful. This is a scoop-shaped piece of metal or plastic which can be pushed down the fish's mouth and into its stomach. By rotating the scoop in the stomach you can withdraw the contents and see what the trout has been eating. Obviously, this exercise should only be conducted on a fish you have killed.

We now come to the vital part of the whole dry fly technique—the relationship between the fly fisherman and his quarry. In order to catch fish you must learn to think like a trout. Do not fool yourself: trout are remarkably able to defend themselves.

In conditions of bright light and clear water the trout can spot the threatening fisherman from a considerable distance. Because of the upstream rule, dry fly fishers start their approach to the fish from the lower end of any suitable part of the water. They work their way upstream, looking for any sign of a rising fish (that is a fish breaking the water and making visible rings on the surface.).

This approach must be extremely cautious. At the first sign of a rising fish, the fisherman must drop to his knees. He must ask himself what the fish is feeding on. Is it nymph, dun or spinner?

The answer is not as simple as might be assumed. We have already learned that nymphs are taken under water, that duns are taken on the surface, and that spinners are also on the surface. Unfortunately, however, nymphs sometimes lie within the surface film, duns are frequently taken when hatching through the surface of the water, and spinners are often taken when in the process of drowning, just below the surface.

How do we tell the difference? Fortunately there are several guides. Consider the time of day. By and large spinners are found on the water in the evening. If there are spinners performing their mating dance along the banks and bushes there is a fair chance that a number of them will have returned to the water to lay their eggs, and will have fallen exhausted on the surface.

If you are fishing in the morning and you can see fish rising, it is not too difficult to spot if duns are being taken from the surface of the water. If they are not, but fish are still disturbing the surface, it is a fairly sure bet that they are taking a hatching nymph (that is a fly emerging from the nymph to the dun stage).

It is frequently difficult to tell if a fish is actually breaking the surface of the water rather than just disturbing it—but it is vitally important to spot the difference since this is the distinction between a rise to a dun and a rise to a nymph. Look for the fish's nose actually breaking the surface. If it does, and you can see a fly on the surface disappear, the fish is taking duns. If you merely see a hump of displaced water, the chances are that the fish has taken a nymph.

Unfortunately, all that I have said so far is only the very beginning of understanding the trout. Put yourself in his position. Where would you like to lie? Where would you feel safe? Where could you get the most food for the least effort? Where would you be least likely to be spotted by predators? Most of all, where could you get all these things and still not be threatened by that enormous shadow that walks up the river bank carrying a fishing rod?

Previously I have only dealt with the ephemera species of the fly family. Here comes a major complication! There are many more species with which the fisher must become familiar. I do not intend to dwell on them all. What I do suggest is that you start your fishing career armed with a copy of A. Courtney Williams' *A Dictionary of Trout Flies*, or with John Goddard's excellent book *Trout Fly Recognition*. The dictionary is basically designed for fly tyers, but whether you tie your own flies or not, it is an invaluable guide to fly fishing entomology.

Next to the Ephemeridae, the most important are sedges (Trichoptera) which the trout consume avidly. These flies are big and meaty, best likened to a moth in appearance. They have large furry bodies and their wings are sloped over their backs, rather like a pitched roof. In their larval state they are not unlike a maggot in appearance. They are known to children as the 'caddis bug'—and indeed they are the larvae of the caddis fly.

Quite apart from the trout's predilection for this fly, it is probably best known for the larva's ability to build its own house. Whatever building materials are available will be used by the caddis larva to construct a shelter to protect itself against predators—ofwhich it has many. Children in classrooms in country districts will have captive caddis bugs in jam jars. The trick is to introduce coloured glass beads into the jar and watch the caddis bug build a protective mosaic home around itself.

As with other water flies, the time comes to hatch into the outside world. The caddis fly emerges through the surface or climbs up reed stems, and becomes a mature fly. After mating it dances and spins over the surface of the water. When it is hatching, or laying eggs, the trout are completely preoccupied with it. What a lovely tasty morsel! It is huge, fluttery and utterly irresistible. Trout will chase them over a considerable area of water, but only because they are big and nourishing—the 'food taken to energy expended' rule still applies.

A further species of importance on some rivers is the stone fly (Perlidae). This is not unlike a house fly in appearance, except that it is longer and thinner—perhaps a compromise between a winged daddy-long-legs and a house fly. It has a long, thin body, but its wings fold flat along its back.

Further, there is the midge. This fly is treated as unimportant on the chalk stream, and probably it is ignored by trout during daylight hours (the only hours when fishing is permitted under normal circumstances). Fish may sometimes be seen to be taking the larvae of the midge (bloodworms) in slack, silty water, but during daylight I have never observed hatching midges being taken.

There are other flies to complicate the normal pattern of those hatching from below the water surface. These are wind-blown flies. They are species which hatch from bankside vegetation and are either blown onto the surface of the water by the wind, or accidentally land on the river when seeking other targets. Probably the most important of these are three species: the hawthorn fly, the black gnat and the daddy-long-legs.

In chalk stream terms the black gnat is the most important. It can be found on the surface of the water at almost any time after April, and trout take it avidly when it is mating. Male and female fall on the water attached tail to tail and the fish cannot resist the double mouthful. The hawthorn fly comes from a similar family to the black gnat, but is much larger and has long, dangly back legs, which make it look incongruous in flight. The hawthorn normally only appears in May and early June (usually when hawthorn bushes are in flower) and in blustery conditions will frequently be found on the surface of the water. The fly's struggles to get free are most attractive to trout. The daddy-long-legs can be found on the water in the latter months of the season and can occasionally be useful to tempt big trout which would not bother rising to a smaller fly.

Below are the artificial flies you should carry in your first season. As you become more experienced you will discard some of my suggestions and replace them with your own favourites. A full list of the flies which I use is contained in Chapter Six of this book.

MAY AND JUNE

There are several patterns of *medium olive*, which hatch throughout the season and are the trout's bread-and-butter fly. Buy size 14 or 16 patterns which are marked 'medium olive' or 'olive dun', or you can use a blue dun, Greenwell's glory, ginger quill or gold ribbed hare's ear. A wetted hare's ear can be used to imitate the nymph of the medium olive, as can the pheasant tail nymph.

At the end of May and beginning of June, on some rivers, the *mayfly* appears. This is one of the largest flies of the fisherman's year and is usually taken greedily by trout. There is a huge selection of flies to choose from. Take local advice about the best patterns for the locality.

The *iron blue dun* is particularly attractive to trout. It is a small fly and its colour is well described by its name. It usually appears on stormy and blustery days towards the end of May and throughout June and July. Buy patterns tied on a No 16 hook—many are tied too large.

For spinner patterns I recommend the pheasant tail spinner or red spinner for the medium olive, and a small pheasant tail spinner (16) or a claret spinner for the iron blue. There are many mayfly spinner patterns, so take local advice.

JULY AND AUGUST

This is the time of *pale watery duns* and *spurwings*. Under most circumstances these two flies can be imitated with the same artificial pattern. They are small flies, and again I would recommend patterns no larger than size 16. Buy patterns under their own name, or a good imitation is the beacon beige. There is also tup's indispensable, but ignore large, garish patterns of the tup with too much pink in the dressing. The fly should be a drab, pale yellow with just a hint of pink in the body. The fly can be used to imitate a dun or a spinner. In the evening the *blue winged olive* comes into its own. It is a fly that is notoriously difficult to imitate but is a great favourite with trout. Perhaps the orange quill is the best generally available pattern, although later in the book I shall give my own pattern for those people who want to tie their own flies, or who can find someone to tie for them. A pheasant tail nymph that is very dark will imitate the nymph, and a pheasant tail spinner or sherry spinner will do for the fourth stage of the fly.

SEPTEMBER
This month sees the return of the medium olives as the principal chalk stream day-time fly.

All the flies I have described so far are of the Ephemeridae family, but you will also need some *sedges*. There is a huge variety of these on offer but only one of any significance to the fisherman, which hatches in April. This is the grannom and it is not found on all chalk streams, but where it does appear it can produce exceptional fishing. For a sedge it is small and should not be bought in a size larger than 14, and is better tied on a No 16 hook. Of the other sedge patterns, I carry just three (best fished from the middle of May onwards): the little red sedge (a marvellous fly for difficult fish), a cinnamon sedge, and Lunn's caperer.

There are several *land-bred flies* that are sold as useful patterns in tackle shops, but there are only three that I find significant: the black gnat, the hawthorn fly and the daddy-long-legs. The hawthorn's season is very short (normally mid-May to the end of the month), but when it does get blown onto the water trout will slash at it hungrily. The black gnat is found on the water through most of the season and trout are very keen on it. The daddy-long-legs can be very useful for bringing up big trout during September.

If you carry the patterns I have described here, you will rarely be stuck for an imitation of the natural fly on the river.

I am sorry to say that we have only scratched the surface of the dry fly fisher's entomology. There are many families, within the Ephemeridae order alone, which must be studied. Different kinds of fly hatch at different times of year and different times of day. The gradual process of learning, together with the books I have recommended, will eventually show you what you have to do in order to catch your fish with the dry fly. Do not be put off, however. It is possible to catch fish from your first day on a dry fly water if you only take the time to study what is happening. I cannot repeat too often that it is all an art of observation, stealth and finesse in casting.

We have now established all the basic principles of dry fly fishing. The flies have been observed in their various stages of development. We have worked out how to study the fish and watch them in their own habitat. We have learned the caution with which they must be approached and we have learned a little of the species that they will eat.

Now comes the time when we approach the water and set out to catch a fish. We have the properly balanced rod, reel and line. Having arrived at the waterside we are looking for one of two things—the rings of the rising or moving fish, or a shape barely detectable under the water, which indicates a fish interested in feeding.

You are looking upstream for any sign of a rise. It is particularly important to search all the water. Look under the bank on which you are standing and scan across. More fish are missed under your own bank than in any other area, so be patient and study carefully. I cannot emphasise too strongly how many fish you will disturb by an incautious step.

Even with polarising glasses, in bright sunlight, trout are hard to see—so proceed with gentle and observant steps! You will curse yourself a dozen times for the fish that will flee from below your feet. Eventually you will spot the betraying rings of a rising fish. STOP!—DROP TO YOUR KNEES!—WATCH! See what the fish is feeding on. Is it nymph, dun or spinner?

It is important to mark the position of the rise next to a feature of bankside vegetation, or some other very close landmark, otherwise it is easy, once having moved, to lose the exact position of the rise. Hands and knees are needed now! Creep up on your quarry until you are in a position where you are confident you can cast a fly comfortably a few feet upstream of the noted place.

Gradually lengthen your line until you are sure that you have enough out to place the fly correctly. This the most crucial point of the dry fly technique. One mistake now and your fish will be gone. It is far better to cast too short than too long. If the fish sees too much of your leader or any of your fly line, it will be frightened away. If you splash your fly on the surface of the water, or cause it to drag unnaturally on the surface, the fish will also take fright.

Eventually your fly lands accurately on the surface of the water and floats down naturally towards the waiting fish. In ideal conditions you will see the fish raise his head and cruise upwards towards your drifting fly. THIS IS SO EXCITING! So what do you do? As a beginner you lift your rod point in anticipation and pull your fly straight out of the fish's mouth. The fish bolts for the nearest weed bed and you wonder what you have done wrong.

It is vitally important that when the fish takes your fly you keep cool. You must wait for his head to go down again. The time between the fish taking the fly and resuming his natural attitude in the water seems interminable, BUT YOU MUST WAIT!

When the fish has resumed a level position a small twist of the wrist in an upwards direction is all that is required to set the hook. If you tug too hard you will either snap the leader at its knot with the fly, or you will pull the fly out of the fish's mouth. The feel for this is learned by experience.

At last you have hooked a fish. It is firmly attached to the end of your line. Now both you and the fish are in a panic—but the trout's natural instinct for self-preservation takes over. If you apply too much pressure to the line the fish will almost certainly leap out of the water, and the chances are that it will land on top of your leader and break it. If the trout jumps, momentarily drop your rod point so that it lands on slack line.

It is essential when playing a fish that you keep your rod pointing skywards. The soft action of the rod will cushion any plunges and rushes the fish makes, and the bend in the rod will ensure that, if the fish turns round, any small slack in the line is taken up as the rod straightens.

One big problem with dry fly fishing is that because you are casting upstream on moving water you are having to pull line through the rod rings as the fly floats down towards you, so that you do not have a large belly in the line between the rod tip and the fly. This means that when the fish takes the fly you normally have a few coils of line round your feet which you have pulled through from the rod between the reel and the first ring.

You must therefore, on hooking the fish, make the best effort you can to recover this slack line back on to the reel as soon as possible. This may be complicated by the fish running towards you as soon as you have hooked it. Under these circumstances you have two choices—to reel in as fast as you can in order to regain direct contact between the rod tip and the fish, or to run backwards down the bank in order to stop the fish gaining slack line. I know of fishermen who use either method (or, under dire circumstances, both).

It must be remembered that more fish are lost when they take advantage of slack line than in almost any other situation. If the fish has control of its head it can suddenly change direction, putting undue stress on the leader; it may dive into weed from where it is often irretrievable, or charge downstream of the fisher where the weight of the water against its flank will often pull the hook loose or break the leader.

When you get a chance, while playing the fish, you should unclip your landing net and unfold it. If you are sure your fish is ready to be landed you should softly dip your net into the water and slowly lead the fish over it. Then, with a gentle movement, you should lift the net under the fish so that its full weight is not taken on the point of the leader.

If the fish is to be killed it is easier to hold it steady while the hook is still attached and the fish is in the net. A deft and firm blow to the top of the head, to the area just to the rear of the eyes, should be enough to dispatch it humanely. Fish that are to be returned to the water should be handled quickly and with wet hands. Before touching the fish, dip your hands in the stream. Take the fish out of your landing net and run your hand down the leader until your fingers find the hook. Remove it with firm backward pressure, at the same time as you apply light pressure to release the hook barb. Gently put the fish back in the water, its head pointing upstream. If the fish tends to roll onto one side, support it gently between your fingers, holding it upright until it has fully recovered and can swim away.

Dry fly fishing is a sport for life and if it were easy it would not keep so many people fascinated for a lifetime. It is therefore important not to be put off by early failures and frustrations. Just keep trying. You will begin to get it right in the end—and you will never stop learning.

NM'90

Chapter Two

Once you know the very basics of dry fly fishing, you are ready to look in more detail at tactics and at some of the trout's idiosyncrasies. I said that the good fisherman develops a sense of how the trout thinks. The better he develops this sense, the more fish he will catch. What seems to make a good fisherman stand out from an indifferent one is his ability to think like a fish and to learn from his own observation.

I see the trout fisher as being rather like Sherlock Holmes. The famous detective had the ability to observe and to learn from that observation. He also had the ability to put himself in the criminal's position. The trout fisher must do the same. When presented with a problem, he should use his observations to form a conclusion. When all those observations are analysed, the combination of them must produce a solution, no matter how unlikely the answer may seem.

I remember one particular fish in an Itchen carrier, which gave me a great deal of pleasure. This fish was in a particularly wild and unkempt area of the fishery and was rising regularly to flies drifting down close to the bank. I could see the fish and the flies quite clearly. Medium olives were drifting downstream and some were taken without hesitation. Before preparing to cast I watched the fish for a while. The hatch of fly was not sufficiently prolific to give the trout a choice within its feeding area, and yet it was not taking every single fly that passed over it. I wondered why. There was no obvious difference between those taken and those refused.

I was able to get quite close to the fish, so the cast that would cover its position would not have to be unduly long, although it was awkward.The fish was lying under my own bank and several small twigs and nettles protruded over the water, threatening to snag the fly if it were not placed carefully. I congratulated myself when the fly landed in the correct position to give it a perfect drift over the fish's lie without being snagged on the bankside vegetation. As the fly floated down the trout raised its head and examined it carefully, as it had done with the naturals. The fly passed right over the fish, but was refused.

I cast again and the result was the same. The fish was still rising to selected naturals, and although it inspected my fly every time I covered the lie, it would not take it. Then one of my casts was wafted over the bankside snags and although the fly landed on the water, the trace ran over the top of a small twig. If I lifted the fly off the water now, the fish would definitely be spooked, so I allowed the fly to continue its drift and hoped that it would not become lodged in the twig when it was pulled over it by the current's drag on the fly line.

Just as the fly was about to reach the fish, the upward drag on the snagged leader lifted it from the surface. There was a boil as the fish jumped at the fly, but it missed and the fly ran over the twig and landed back on the water behind the trout. The fish seemed unperturbed and continued to feed selectively as before. This time I watched the naturals even more minutely. Suddenly I noticed the difference between those being taken and those that were ignored. The fish was only eating the flies that were moving as they floated down on the current. In every case the ones that were immobile were ignored, but those that were struggling to get their balance on the surface or to rid themselves of their nymphal shuck or casing were taken without hesitation.

My next casts were specifically aimed to get the leader across the bankside twig. Eventually I was successful, and as the fly was lifted off the surface by the snagged leader, the trout rose and I hooked it. I landed a beautiful native Itchen trout weighing a shade under two-and-a-half pounds. Although the fish itself was a delight to look at, my glow of satisfaction came from having used wile and observation to fool an extremely fussy trout.

This attraction to movement is a feature of all trout, and when fish are relying entirely on movement to trigger their feeding routine they can be very hard to tempt. In Chapter Five I describe how to tie flies with hackle-point wings. These wings give the illusion of movement and can be very deadly.

Perhaps the most difficult natural fly to imitate is the blue winged olive. I am sure that this is due primarily to the amount of movement this fly makes while hatching. If you watch the species closely you will see that there are very few occasions when the duns are still. They struggle violently while hatching out of the nymphal shuck, and once they have hatched into the dun stage they continue to move their wings and legs as they float down on the surface. They attempt to fly continuously until finally they manage to get airborne. I am sure that this movement is what makes them so attractive to trout. Their struggling and fluttering will often entice a trout to move several yards from its lie in order to capture one.

This is also borne out by the rise-form to the blue winged olive. The rise is quite explosive, with the fly often being taken while the fish is on the turn. The rise to a sedge is also an untidy affair—probably for the same reason. Sedges also struggle and flutter on the surface and the fish makes a wild grab, fearing that the quarry will escape unless it is caught quickly.

The rise-form can therefore be a guide to the species of fly being consumed but, more importantly, can also give an indication that the fish is only rising to moving flies. If, for instance, it is obvious that a fish is rising to medium olives, because they are the only species on the water at the time or because you can see a fish actually taking them, but the rises are more violent than usual, there is a fair chance that the fish is showing preference for the ones that are moving.

Fishing tactics and fly patterns can be altered to take advantage of this.

Another interesting feature of feeding trout is their preference for flies on just one side of them. This is sometimes caused by a fish being blind in one eye, so that it can only see flies passing on the sighted side. But I have witnessed this behaviour in many trout which have two perfectly good eyes.

Once again it is an occasion where observation is important. Sometimes the preference to rise to just one side is caused simply by the flow of the current, which is bringing most of the food to a particular side of the fish's lie. But I have known occasions when duns and nymphs to the right of a fish have been ignored, while every one that passed to the left was intercepted. Why trout should display this preference I do not know, but good observation can mean the capture of a fish that would otherwise seem impossible to tempt.

There is another tactic for difficult fish, first described by G. E. M. Skues, that famous Itchen fisherman and author. He noted that fish which were being particularly difficult to tempt with either a dry fly or a nymph could sometimes be persuaded to take a fly if it dropped immediately over them. The normal dry fly cast is aimed so that the fly lands two to three feet upstream of the fish, but this does give the trout time to examine the fly quite carefully before deciding whether to accept or reject it. If the fly is dropped right above the fish's position, it does not have nearly so much time to make up its mind and will quite often turn and slash at the fly instinctively, for fear of losing it.

Observation is also vital in determining whether a trout is anxious to feed. There are two principal indications to look for. First, the fish should be high in the water, and second, it should be 'on the fin'. This phrase is a perfect description for a fish that looks alert. Its fins, particularly the pectorals, stand out from the body, the tail has a purposeful wave in its movement and the fish's head moves from side to side, searching the water for any morsel being swept down by the current.

Fish displaying these symptoms will often be seen to dart forward to intercept a nymph, and they will quite often lift their heads to examine some passing piece of detritus. Although frequently there may be no sign of hatching flies, the angler should take heart if he sees these signs. Almost invariably it means that a good hatch of fly is about to start.

There will remain many occasions when, no matter how good your observation and knowledge of the water, trout will be seen rising when there is apparently no hatch of fly, and many others when you will see a rise-form but are unable to see the fish. It is on these occasions that you must use your Sherlock Holmes tactics.

The first thing to bear in mind is the time of year and the time of day. You know what flies are likely to be on the water according to the month and the weather; you should also know in which state of development they are likely to be, as dictated by the time of day. The first thing to do, therefore, is to look in the air, on the water, in the water and to examine bankside foliage. Unless visibility is very poor, it should be possible to see any of the ordinary duns floating down on the surface. If there aren't any, you will have to assume that the fish is either eating something so small that you can't see it, or is rising to something that is either trapped in the surface film or just below the surface. If it were taking anything lying deeper there would be no apparent rise-form on the surface.

Even if the trout's victim is very small and you cannot get close enough to the fish to see what it is feeding on, you still have the ability to study the water closely as it flows past your position. Small black gnats can be very hard to see at any distance; so can spinners if they are partially drowned. Even harder to spot are inert nymphs which may be floating past, just below the surface. If you are to catch the fish it is important that your inspection of the surface is minute and painstaking. If there are very small black gnats on the surface the chances are that your trout is feeding on these. The same applies to spinners. If you can spot spinners in the surface film, try to pull one out of the water so that you can examine it closely and match it with an appropriate pattern in your fly box. It is also worth remembering that some spinners actually climb down reed stems and bridge supports to lay their eggs. Some of these are swept away by the current and are trapped below the surface film where they are particularly hard to detect.

Once you have ruled out all the main possibilities, the only remaining option must be the solution to the problem. 'It's elementary, dear Watson!'

I particularly mentioned the possibility of drowned spinners because of an incident quite early on in my fly fishing experience. I had seen spinners dancing above the banks and had found one or two sheltering under the broader-leaved bankside plants. There was a particular fish rising close to some sedges that lined the opposite bank. Its rises were just the tiniest sips that hardly disturbed the surface. I put on a pheasant tail spinner, oiled it carefully, and cast to the fish. Although I covered the fish time after time and it continued rising, it would not take the fly. The next cast was a bit fumbled and the fly hit the surface more firmly than it had done previously. The extra impetus pushed the spinner through the surface film, and as it drifted over the trout's position I saw the sipping rise and tightened. I hooked and landed a nice trout.

Armed with this experience I moved upstream and eventually saw another fish performing the same sipping rise. I wetted the spinner in the water and when I covered the fish the fly was taken first time. That evening I took several fish, all on the drowned spinner.

About three weeks after this experience, when I thought I had solved the problem of difficult spinner rises, I was fishing the same length of river and saw the same rise—that little sip under the bank, which can be heard almost better than it can be seen. There is the quietest 'smack', like the sound of a ping-pong ball being dropped gently from a few inches on to a marble floor. This is where observation comes in again. The angler must scan the water carefully in order to see the rise. It is no more than the smallest dimple, often almost imperceptible in the confusion of ripples that run under a bank.

On this occasion I wetted the fly in my mouth and cast to the fish. The cast was accurate but there was no take. I tried several times more but there was still no result. What was I doing wrong? It had worked so well before. When drawing the fly off in order to recast I realised that quite a length of the leader was also submerged. In a rush it all came to me. If the leader begins to sink, the fly passes under the fish and in these circumstances it will not be taken. The leader needs to be greased right down to the fly, so that the fly is only just under the surface, trapped below the film just like the naturals.

There is another moral to this story: you should never believe everything you are told. I was fishing at this time on the same water as quite a well-known fisherman who had the reputation as an expert on the dry fly. He told me that it was important that the spinner should be high floating and should always be kept well water-proofed.

Anyone who sees for themselves a spent spinner on the water cannot fail to notice that even those that are freshly spent lie flat on the surface or are actually trapped within the film. I am glad that my accidental discovery enabled me to appreciate that this particular 'guru' did not know as much as I had been led to believe.

Don't misunderstand me. There is no substitute for local advice, and the observations of one's fishing companions can be very valuable, but always believe the evidence of your own eyes in preference to fishing-hut gossip. Dogma can mean many missed fish and wasted opportunities. So often the very people who tell you how much they know about fishing turn out to be ignorant on really basic facts. It is just like life in general, really, because it is not until you have gained your own experience (and prejudices) that you realise that in most issues there is no black and white.

It is this reliance on the evidence of your own eyes that will gradually lead to you become a good fisherman rather than an average one. I am not a betting man, but I can see certain parallels between betting and fishing. The average punter places his bet either on a whim or because he has heard gossip that a particular horse is a winner. The punters who do better are those who study form or bother to go to the gallops and use their own stopwatches to monitor a horse's performance. The same applies to fishing. Anglers who study form consistently catch more fish than those who take pot luck and follow indifferent advice offered by people with little knowledge. Anything you can do to shorten the odds on the river must be to your advantage and you have an advantage over the punter because you have access to many of the facts just by using your own eyes.

I think that part of the whole business of fishing is to have an affinity with your quarry. Philosophically this amounts to much more than a will to catch fish. It is to have a real feeling for the trout; to know how it feels; to know, if you were the fish, where you would feel secure and contented; to know what particular kind of food you would find attractive.

I know so many fishermen who become furious because they have not caught fish when others have. They get tangles, cannot find the right fly, become frustrated and generally fish with more and more desperation as the day goes on. They are their own worst enemies. They are making life so difficult for themselves. If they could only be happy just to stay beside the river and see the fish they catch as a bonus, they would catch many more fish.

There is a lovely saying: 'The worst day fishing is better than the best day working.' I am permanently surprised by those who regard a day's fishing as just another day's work. They must compete for fish as they compete for contracts, and some even apply accountants' rules—they have to catch an equal value of fish to the cost of a season's fishing. I know of one who even adds in the cost of petrol to get him to the fishery—God help him!

For many years I was privileged to fish at Abbotts Barton, which formed part of the old fishery that was Skues' stamping ground on the Itchen. Despite the fact that this water has been taken over by the progress of our modern age (an industrial estate now flanks the opposite bank of the main river and the traffic roar from the extension of the M3 wafts across a neighbouring hillside), some features remain the same.

Some of the best fishing at Abbotts Barton used to be on the Barton Carrier, which runs through the west side of the fishery, following an approximately parallel course to the main river. It is one of the disasters resulting from modern water authority management that this carrier is now heavily silted from end to end through Abbotts Barton (and no doubt throughout the rest of its length) due to lack of flow.

The bottom end of this carrier (as the limits now stand) was described in Skues' book *The Chalk Stream Angler* as the 'Haunt of the Aunt Sallies'. Skues' description of the particular bend was as true in 1985 as it had been when his book was published in 1932. This bend always held a trout of considerable size, which was protected by willows that overhung the water from the opposite bank as it swept through a deep bending pool before beginning its descent through the meadows flanking what is now a local recreation ground. This pool provided the perfect lie.

There was one member at Abbotts Barton, the club secretary at that time, named Bob Schröder, who was about the same age as my father. We just seemed to get on; it was as though the generation gap did not exist. I was in my thirties and he in his late sixties. We talked fishing frequently over lunch in the fishing-hut and knew each other well enough to be able to make fun of one another's idiosyncrasies.

A pattern evolved in our fishing timetables: we would each fish by ourselves in the morning, meet for lunch and set off together in the afternoon. These afternoons were usually spent fishing for the most difficult trout on the water, fish which inhabited various lies all over the fishery and were normally large trout that everyone had tried unsuccessfully to catch. Either the line had broken, or the fish were in such difficult positions that they were really hard to reach with a fly.

At the head of the pool which Skues called the 'Haunt of the Aunt Sallies', about a yard from the far bank, was a large mound of starwort. Behind this weedbed lay a trout of considerable proportions—it was reckoned to weigh around three pounds. Above this fish was a willow, one branch of which had leaves that fluttered within about a foot of the surface. The fly had to be dropped just above the starwort, but this manoeuvre was complicated by the overhanging leaves. The fly had to land gently, but just at the moment when the cast was straightening, so that it was sufficiently close to the surface not to be snagged in the tree.

Trails of nylon were suspended from the twigs as evidence of the number of members who had chanced a fly at this most tempting fish. I must point out that this wise creature was also extremely sensitive to the activities of fishermen on the opposite bank. Back-casts were impeded by tall reeds behind, but kneeling was essential if the fish was not to sink out of sight into the roots that guarded a secret hiding-place under the far bank.

One afternoon found Bob Schröder and myself in the fishing-hut. We had taken lunch and were feeling generally at peace with the world after a glass or two of beer and a very small whisky each, poured from the 'smallest flask in England' which Bob kept in his fishing bag. We decided that our 'Aunt Sally' for the afternoon should be the fish described above.

When we arrived at our destination there was a stiffish breeze coming from our right, which not only occasionally lifted the offending leaves from above the lie of the fish, but might also serve to propel the fly to a position over the starwort where, all things being equal, the current would carry the delicious-looking artificial morsel over the head of the waiting trout. The fish was well up in the water, obviously 'on the fin' and looking for food. Under the circumstances it was typical of Bob's generosity that he offered me first 'chuck'.

The fly of the morning had been a medium olive, and there was still a trickle of them passing over Aunt Sally as she lay downstream of the weedbed. She was not taking every fly that drifted overhead, but occasionally a minute adjustment of the pectoral fins would lift her gently in the current and she would allow herself to be carried backwards while she studied the fly minutely before opening her mouth. A tiny whirlpool of water formed above her mouth and the fly would subside between the waiting jaws. A lazy wag of the tail and Aunt Sally was back in position, ruminating on the small mouthful she had just intercepted.

My own pattern of medium olive was already attached to my leader and I lengthened line in order to cover the fish. I shall not dwell on the number of times I was caught up behind, nor the number of times Bob retrieved the fly from the feathered fronds of the reeds, at the same time buckling the heads of those likely to be a nuisance on the next cast.

Eventually, with the help of the breeze, it all worked perfectly. The fly landed just above the starwort and began its drift downstream. Up came the trout's head and Aunt Sally once again repeated the actions she had gone through with the naturals that had drifted over her— but with one exception. Her minute inspection of the fly did not satisfy her and she let it drift downstream unheeded while she regained her position. This rejection and the two that followed were enough to tell me that the fish did not want my pattern.

'You have a go,' I said to Bob. His favourite ginger quill was dispatched over the fish with similar results. On each occasion she followed the fly and was obviously sufficiently interested to inspect it carefully. We both tried several other patterns without success, and eventually decided to rest and watch for a while.

As we watched I twice saw the trout duck sideways to intercept a nymph. 'Perhaps it would be less fussy about a nymph,' I said. Bob shrugged and pulled the sort of face that suggested we were wasting our time, but I tied on a small dark hare's ear nymph. When it landed in the right position the trout followed but did not take it. 'You'll never catch it,' Bob said after several more casts. And that was the magic phrase. The fish opened and closed its mouth, I tightened and there was a splash. The line was hissing through the rod rings.

As he netted out a fish of two pounds fourteen ounces, Bob said: 'I knew that if I said that you'd catch it!' But I am still not convinced.

It could be claimed that pure persistence caught this fish, but a degree of observation and deduction was also involved. Although the trout was obviously taking duns, it was not taking them all, and I have noticed that a fish that is particularly choosy over a pattern of dry fly will frequently be persuaded to take a nymph.

Part of the art of observation is the reading of rise-forms. I have already mentioned two of them—the excited slash at a moving fly and the tiny sipping rise made by fish taking spent spinners under banks. There are several other rises which can give a good guide to the species of fly being taken.

I wrote an article on rise-forms which was published in *Trout and Salmon* magazine in July 1986, and this caused some controversy at the time. Anyone who has been fishing for any length of time cannot fail to have noticed the so-called 'head-and-tail' rise. This is an inaccurate description of the rise-form, because it leaves out the dorsal fin from the sequence. If one watches a fish rising in this style it will be noticed that first its head appears out of the water, then its dorsal fin, and finally its tail. It is a sort of lazy porpoise roll. Whenever I had witnessed this particular rise-form it had been made by a fish obviously in no hurry to secure its prey.

Using my Sherlock Holmes reasoning, I concluded that this was a rise to a spent spinner, and on most occasions when I witnessed the rise-form I subsequently caught the fish in question on one of my spinner imitations. The head-and-tail rise is most often performed by a fish that is lying out in open water. Why this should be so, I do not understand. But fish taking spinners close to the bank more usually make the sipping rise I have already described.

A month or two after my article appeared, another one was published in which the writer, Timothy Benn, claimed that the head-

and-tail rise was invariably made by fish that were rising to midge pupae. His article put forward the theory that river fishermen in general had ignored the possibilities offered by midge imitations. He argued that fish that were difficult to rise were frequently to be caught on a fly representing the midge pupa.

While I was interested in his theory generally on midges in rivers, I was annoyed that he should suggest that head-and-tailing fish were always rising to midge pupae. My own observations had proved to me conclusively that head-and-tailing fish could frequently be caught on spinner imitations. I reproduce this argument here not as an academic point but because it led to a further observation on rise-forms which may be very relevant in determining the species of fly being taken by trout.

Some weeks later I was having lunch outside the fishing-hut at Abbotts Barton and was looking up the Barton Carrier, watching a fish that was head-and-tailing in the centre of the stream. This fish rose frequently and was often cast to by members who had spotted the rise from the fishing-hut. However, it had proved impossible to fool with any imitation in my possession. As I watched the fish rise again I saw the usual pattern as first its head, then its dorsal fin, and finally its tail appeared. Just before the tip of its tail disappeared below the surface, I noticed an interesting feature: the tail was given a leisurely and gentle wave.

At this time I had been in correspondence with Timothy Benn. His most recent letter had asked me for some observations for an article he was planning. I told him of the tail-waving trout and how I had seen this feature before but had failed to take note of it. 'Can it be,' I wrote, 'that we have been talking about two different rise-forms?'

My remarks were published in Timothy's subsequent article, and it turned out that the famous and erudite fisherman John Goddard had mentioned the tail-wave in his book *The Trout and the Fly*, which had been published some time before. He had attributed the rise to fish that were taking spinners or small duns, but subsequent thoughts after the book's publication led him to believe that they could have been taking midge pupae.

The final chapter in this correspondence came with the publication of a letter from Gordon Mackie, another well-known southern fisher-man. He had noted that the tail-wave only seemed to be displayed by fish rising in relatively slow-flowing water, and then only by fish that were stocked. Native fish or those in fast-flowing water, he suggested, did not show the wave when head-and-tailing. His letter recommended a fly tied with dark deer hair on a No 14 hook, with the fur clipped close to the hook shank.

All the fishermen I have mentioned are good observers of fish, with the result that all had remarked on the tail-wave. What is noteworthy is the different solutions that have been proposed in order to solve the problem. It's back to Sherlock Holmes again!

To return to the subject of rise-forms in general, I think it can safely be assumed that trout head-and-tailing without the final wave are likely to be taking spinners. You must form your own conclusions over those exhibiting the wave. Fish sipping under banks, particularly in the evening, are also usually taking spinners.

Violent rises, particularly under bridges, trees or in sluice pools and other dark places are most likely to be fish taking sedges, although a similar rise in open water can, as already discussed, be caused by a rise to any active fly. Skues noted that fish rising to the blue winged olive left a sort of 'kidney-shaped whorl' on the surface of the water. I have not noticed this shape quite as he described it, but there is no question that, for some reason, perhaps because the fly is captured as the fish turns, there is frequently a double circle left on the surface after the blue winged olive is captured. ·

Very often, particularly in May and early June, there will be medium olives, iron blues and pale wateries on the river at the same time, and when there are bright reflections it is sometimes hard to tell which particular species is being selected by the trout. Some guide may be obtained from the speed of the rise. In my experience, of the three flies, the iron blues spend the shortest time on the surface between hatching and flying. It follows that the fastest rise will therefore normally be to the iron blue. The slowest and most leisurely rise is normally to the medium olive. Pale wateries are frequently taken with a sort of sip—not as slight as the sip to a spinner, but generally with less water movement than that occasioned by rises to the medium olive.

If there is black gnat on the water as well as pale wateries it is possible to confuse the two rise-forms. They are very similar, but because of the profile of the black gnat it is unlikely that the fisher will be confused by the two, even against a bright reflection.

Larger flies present no problem. They are seen easily enough to work out whether they are being taken. As for spinners, there is a real difficulty. Because they are found more frequently in the evening when the light is bad and because they often lie within the surface, the rise-forms to all of them are similar, being either a sip or a head-and-tail pattern. You can reduce your odds by studying those dancing above the banks, and if you have been on the water all day you will normally know the predominant fly that has hatched. At times of prolific hatches I am afraid you will have to use trial and error by casting various patterns to rising fish, in the hope that one of them will work. Fortunately the range of useful spinner patterns is limited, so an initial wrong selection can usually be substituted for the right fly after only a couple of false starts.

Chapter Three

Perhaps one of the most vital aspects of dry fly fishing is the ability to see fish while not allowing them to see you. Those who are not used to seeing fish are frequently amazed by those who can see them, but as with most fly fishing techniques it is a knack that is relatively easily learned.

The first essential is to study the water carefully. Every stretch of flowing water has its own pattern of currents, ripples and weed growth. This pattern must be studied to become familiar with the way everything moves—so that you are aware of the overall 'shape' of the movement of the water past the various obstructions. When your eyes have grown used to the pattern, the occasionally anomaly will appear. You will see a movement that is not in keeping with the general pattern. More often than not this movement will be a trout. Sometimes its tail will move in the opposite sense to the movement of the weed around it, or at others it will be moving with a different frequency. Quite suddenly an area of the stream that seemed to be devoid of fish will turn out to be holding several trout.

Knowing where to look is also a help. Any interruption in the flow of current is a potential lie for a fish, but there are two other prerequisites to make it desirable. It must provide security from predators and it must have a good food supply. Look for the places that supply these requirements and do not be put off if at first there are apparently no fish there. Many a time I have been unable to spot a fish in what seems to be a good lie, only to see one bolt for cover as soon as my incautious step has given away my presence.

Frequently fish will lie in runs between weedbeds, which makes them hard to spot from the bank, but careful observation will often reveal the tip of a tail appearing occasionally above the fronds. Another good indicator, when trout are lying with their heads just out of a weedbed, is the opening and closing of their mouths to intercept nymphs or shrimps. The flash can be as clear as sema-phore. It is remarkable how white the inside of a trout's mouth is.

In their book *The Trout and the Fly*, John Goddard and Brian Clarke mentioned visible patches worn in the river bed where it had been scoured by a fish's tail. This may be a good indication on rivers where there is a thin covering of silt over a gravel or chalk bed, but in my experience it does not give away lies over a clean bottom, or those with a thick layer of silt or mud. I am sure the best way to spot fish is to learn where they are likely to lie and then to look for them. I have already mentioned the importance of thinking like a fish; if you do this you are half-way to seeing them.

It can pay handsome dividends just to watch the way trout behave. It is very difficult, if you have a fishing rod in your hand, to contain your enthusiasm sufficiently to sit and watch a fish without attempt-ing to catch it, but the rewards will be great. If you have insufficient self-restraint it may be a good idea to spend the off-season looking for fish and then spending a while watching them.

You will notice, when you are used to watching old friends in familiar lies, that trout seem to have at least two favoured positions. The first is the visible feeding station and the other is a bolt-hole among the weeds. If you intentionally frighten a fish you have been watching you will see that it usually makes for the same sanctuary, often no more than a yard or two from its feeding lie and sometimes adjacent to it. If there is no fish in a familiar lie or in a position that looks ideal, it is worth sitting down quietly on the bank and waiting to see if a fish appears from a nearby refuge to take up a feeding stance. Trout that are anxious to feed will normally return to the lie within ten minutes or so of being frightened.

While familiarity with the water you are fishing is a great advantage, it is not essential in order to find fish. In the old days of the chalk streams, the purists would only fish the rise. Fortunately this particular item of etiquette has been discontinued on the rivers I fish, so that now it is acceptable to look in the water for fish which may be taking nymphs, and to fish to them, even though they are not rising to dry flies.

I can see why the etiquette became established. On one river that I fished regularly it was not uncommon to see anglers walking along the bank peering down into the water below their feet. In these circumstances, any self-respecting trout will bolt for cover long before the offending fisher is upon them. This is a very selfish action by the fisherman, because not only does it spoil the fishing for anyone who may be following him, but it can ultimately, if practised often enough, cause fish to give up more open lies in favour of somewhere more secure.

The trout is well aware that the fisherman is the most dangerous of all predators. I remember one member who, every time he fished, used to walk bolt upright along the banks, peering into the water. Eventually other fishermen would say that there was no point in going to a particular beat on the fishery because it had just been patrolled by that member. The sad thing was that the person in question caught very few fish himself, quite apart from spoiling things for others.

The way to find fish is to set up station in a place concealed from the trout. Make yourself comfortable and then begin to study the pattern of the water. It is vital to study the water nearest you while bearing the trout's requirements in mind, so look for good potential lies and then concentrate on these. Study each lie carefully for a resident fish. Remember that your initial approach may have frightened a fish, so give it time to come out of its bolt-hole and take up station. I cannot stress too often how studying the water will reveal fish in an area that at first glance seemed to be devoid of all life.

Remember the old efficiency rule—that a trout, in order to grow and put on weight, needs to eat more calories than it burns, so it will generally lie in places where the least possible energy is expended on remaining there. Any interruption in the current can therefore offer a suitable lie. The pressure wave that builds up in front of an obstruction can be used by the fish to hold it against the current, so that it simply has to use its tail and pectoral fins to keep it in balance or to change its attitude in the water. Fish will lie both in front of and behind these obstructions. If they do not use the pressure wave at the front they will take advantage of the backwash of the circulating eddy behind. Generally, the bigger the disruption to the current, the more attractive the lie.

Obviously a prime consideration is the proliferation of food. There is no point in a fish holding station in a comfortable lie if the current does not carry food to it, so you are also looking for features that will funnel food from a relatively large area of the river into a reasonably small space. When you have found a lie that meets these criteria it is usual that it will be inhabited by a fish.

Many thousands of words have been written about the way a trout sees. Highly qualified scientists have put up a great number of theories on fish vision, and the most popularly accepted is probably the 'window' supposition. Briefly, it is held that a trout sees through the surface of the water via a conical area, with the point of the cone drawn from the top of the eye. On this basis, therefore, it is assumed that a fish lying near the surface sees through a smaller 'window' than one lying deeper. It is held that the area of the water's surface outside the window acts as a mirror, so that the fish can only see reflections of its own world in the area outside the circle of the 'window'.

I am afraid I beg to differ. In my experience, fish near the surface can see a far greater distance and at a wider angle than those lying deep. It must be remembered that this cannot be judged simply by the fact that fish near the surface take fright much earlier than those lying deep. Deep-lying fish, I am sure, feel more secure than those close to the surface. Although I partly base my judgement on 'frightenability', a more important fact is that fish lying near the surface will frequently move a greater distance in order to intercept a fly. I have seen fish lying near the surface that have dashed several yards and leapt from the water to catch a fluttering sedge. Trout lying deep often travel relatively large distances to intercept nymphs, but will normally only rise to floating flies that are relatively close overhead. The implication is that the deep-lying trout only sees flies in a fairly small area above it.

Further, fish lying near the surface will often be frightened by a false cast which, according to the 'window' theory, they should not have been able to see at all because it was hidden by the mirror—despite the fact that the mirror must frequently be broken by ripples.

How is it that under ˌertain conditions of light fish seem to be able to see more than twice the distance that they can at other times? No, in my view the 'window' theory is a carefully and academically thought-out argument that is not valid in practice.

In both 1989 and 1990 the lack of rain meant that fish, as a result of low water levels, had to lie closer to the surface than usual, and I don't think I have ever known them so jittery. Yet for the first time during those seasons I witnessed some fish covering relatively huge distances to intercept surface fly which, in theory, should have been way beyond their area of vision.

I also suffered, time and again, from putting down regularly rising fish just by lifting my rod. Under normal conditions I would have had no qualms about approaching within ten yards of a rising fish. In 1989 and 1990 I had to cast from more than fifteen yards, and still managed to put some of the trout down. If you'll pardon the pun, there is more to trout vision than meets the eye.

Some of the quirks, however, can be predicted and used to advantage. Fishermen are frequently warned about putting themselves between the fish and the sun. Don't believe a word of it! I hooked one of the most difficult trout I have ever known by using the sun to my advantage. On a carrier on the Itchen there was a low bridge, no more than eighteen inches above the surface of a fast-flowing stream. Lying beneath this bridge was a trout of majestic proportions. When he chose to feed he would rise under the bridge with a loud and frustrating splash. I waited until the wind was perfect to aid the fly's propulsion under the bridge, but that fish knew exactly the limit of my wind-assisted casting ability! His rise was always just six inches beyond my range.

I studied that fish. I discovered that when he was not used to seeing people about, he would drop back and happily take flies about a foot downstream of the bridge. I must explain the geography. This particular carrier was no more than twelve feet wide as it flowed under the bridge. Just twenty feet or so downstream of the bridge the stream made a sharp turn to the right. This meant that an angler standing on the bank and attempting to cast to the fish, without allowing his line to be caught in bankside vegetation, could not stand farther back than, say, 25 feet of the fish's lie. Anyone getting that close was spotted immediately by the wily trout.

Now, here was the dilemma: did you crawl on your hands and knees until you were in a position to cast, only to make the fish bolt under the bridge as soon as you raised your rod? Did you stand so far back that half your line was entangled in the bankside vegetation, so that you only got one cast and then had to put the fish down in order to release your fly? Or did you find some other subterfuge that gave you mastery over this seemingly impossible trout?

On a particularly sunny day, I again crept up on this trout. I had already given him up as hopeless but I could not resist another try. He always saw me, and always shot under the bridge. This morning the sun was high and behind me. It was sufficiently high not to cast my shadow more than a couple of feet across the water. I crept into my normal position and raised my rod, fully expecting His Majesty to give his usual imperious flick of the tail and disappear under the bridge. Wonder of wonders! As I raised my rod he lifted his head and sucked down a natural succulent medium olive that happened to be passing over him.

I gave two false casts and dropped the fly just right. Up came His Majesty's head and down went my fly. A flick of the wrist and the fish was hooked. I blush to tell you that he went straight up under the bridge, out the other side and broke my line—but I had fooled him!

This experience taught me that a fish cannot see a fisherman coming out of the sun. It is like the old fighter pilots' adage—'beware of the Hun in the sun'. If you have the sun immediately above your head, the fish cannot see you—it is blinded; anything within the halo of sunlight is invisible. I have since used this trick on many fish. In some cases you can almost stand on their tails!

Another problem with light is that of reflected light, particularly flash, either from the fishing rod or from the trace. The rod I use is an eight-and-a-half foot Hardy carbon fibre. Despite the preachings of Skues and many others, I cannot bring myself to put a matt finish on a rod that is so beautifully turned out. To cover up the depth of the two-coloured whippings, and the patterns in the carbon fibre windings of the rod itself, would be more than I could bear. Even if I frighten the odd trout, I am afraid I cannot bring myself to ruin the beautiful finish of my rod.

There have been days when I have watched other fishermen across the meadows and have been dazzled by the flash of their rods from half a mile away. There is no question that on occasion fish within a few yards must see the same thing. Skues advocated a matt finish rod, preferably painted a light blue-grey colour, as camouflage against the sky. It is significant that his 'world's best rod' (as he called it), which is in the Fly Fishers' Club in London, is finished in a natural gloss varnish!

Another reflection to avoid is that from bright clothing. Some of the more traditional fishermen on the hallowed chalk streams believe in dressing up to go fishing. While their moleskin breeks and tweed jackets are normally of a sombre hue, many favour Tattersall shirts, which carry a brown or green check on a white background. Although these shirts may suit the country gentleman's outfit, the white background of the shirt can be seen from miles away.

Coarse fishermen by and large favour army combat jackets and trousers. Although they are suitably sombre, on a hot day they can be unbearable. I usually wear an olive green-coloured shirt and similar-coloured cotton or denim trousers. My fishing waistcoat is a similar colour. Because of my habit of climbing under bridges or kneeling in boggy patches, I prefer not to worry too much about sartorial elegance, but instead favour such practicalities as comfort and easy washing.

Perhaps the most important consideration is personal comfort. The good fly fisherman will spend a great deal of time crouching and watching, so it is important that his clothing does not bind in the crotch, under the arms, in the backs of the knees or round the ankles, and is not easily snagged on brambles and twigs. Loose weave sweaters can be a nightmare if you get a hook caught in the centre of the back. Thick seams finishing the legs of trousers can cause severe soreness round the ankles when waders or wellingtons are worn.

While on the subject of suitable clothing, I must mention the fishing waistcoat. Being a chalk stream man I am, in some respects, a traditionalist, so for many years I carried a game bag, rather than succumb to that rather *avant-garde* invention from the United States, the 'fishing vest'. When my bag finally got past its best I went to look at some new ones. I am not usually mean, but have you seen the price of them? So I looked at some waistcoats instead. My bag was a good quality one, but even so the leather pocket straps had all formed spirals like watch springs. The metal hinges on the webbing had turned sideways so that the shoulder strap could no longer be adjusted and, no matter what I did, the bag would never stay far enough round my back not to impede some of my movements when I was fishing.

I went into the waistcoat business in some detail. I looked at several and finally settled for the Hardy Bros one. It was not cheap and had fewer pockets than some, but it was comfortable and had enough pockets to contain everything that I normally carry for a day beside the river. I have now had the same waistcoat for seven years. All the pocket press studs still work. The zips on the front and the other pockets all still work and have not come unattached. There was a rather large loop at the back of the neck that was designed for hanging it up, but that tickled my neck so I chopped it off, and the landing net ring at the waist was in the wrong position for my net— but apart from that its performance has been exemplary and it still has plenty of wear left in it. One of the few disadvantages is that you cannot carry fish in it. I believe that the large back pocket was designed for this, but in view of the fact that the fish could be held close to your body for a considerable time, I have chosen not to use it for this purpose.

The solution to the landing net problem was solved by a fishing friend. The ring on my jacket was at such a height that, when I knelt down, the folded handle of my net would push against the ground and silently unclip the net. When I eventually got into a fish, I would find that my net was missing and I would have to land the fish by hand. After landing the fish or not, as the case might be, I would then have to search the river bank for my missing net.

The clip on a landing net is suspect at the best of times, so what was needed was a belt through which the folded handle could be threaded. My fishing friend wore a belt rather like a diagonal body sash (Order of the Garter style). He simply pushed the folded net handle through the body side of the belt, allowing the net frame to hang the other side. I found a suitable length of webbing to fit my body and now carry my net in the same way. It can be withdrawn from the belt with a simple one-handed action and I am now never separated from my net unless my absentmindedness causes me to leave it on the bank after netting out a fish.

Important though all this is, we must go back to the subject of light. There are certain days when every fish in the river seems to take fright at any movement. This is particularly true in the late summer and early autumn. At this time of year the river is usually at its clearest, which partly explains the fish having jitters, but much more important, I am sure, is the quality of the light.

Although many trout fishermen abhor bright sunlight, in my experience this is not the problem. Highly defined shadows can offer the angler a chance to hide among shadows and even blend into his surroundings if he is in part light and part shade. No, the real problem is during periods of bright, diffused light. A high, thin cloud cover can be far more troublesome than direct sunlight, and even some cloudy days have a sort of monochrome universality of light that makes it hard for the fisherman to hide.

It is on these occasions that the utmost wariness must be exercised when fishing. The fisherman can often hide in front of objects, as well as behind them. An area of shadow behind him can be as useful as a bush in front him, and far less restrictive. What must be avoided is to be silhouetted against a bright background, or to be a bright object reflecting light when surrounded by a dark background. This is what makes diffused light so difficult to cope with; it seems to enhance the trout's vision and remove solids that can provide cover.

I have frequently read that fishing is poor when there is mist, particularly the evening mist that rises from the water when the cooler evenings of autumn arrive. I think that the problem is probably not so much the mist as the diffused light that comes with it.

Although flies may continue to hatch and fish may continue to rise in the mist, the fisherman is far more easily seen by the fish, so that they stop rising while he is near.

Although the afterglow of a sunset at the end of a hot day will often produce superb evening fishing, I have found that fish can be more wary in this light than at any other time of day. They seem to be very sensitive to the finest leader on the surface and often stop rising when the angler first lifts his rod to begin casting. Although the intensity of light is much reduced, the evening afterglow has that same diffused effect as those monochrome days of bright, hazy light.

So often in the evening I have been excited by the sight of the first blue winged olives drifting down on the water. The fish begin to rise steadily and solidly and it looks as though nothing will put them off their evening feast. Exercising extreme caution, the angler creeps up on a rising trout. From a position on his knees he starts false casting to work out enough line to cover the nearest rising fish with his orange quill. There is no give-away bow wave of a departing fish—the trout just stops rising. Another fish a few yards higher up is within reach and is still rising. A few false casts are made to gain a little more line while the fish continues to rise. The first cast is perfect, with just the tip of the leader covering the fish. The fly cocks beautifully and drifts over the position of the last rise, but there is no response. The fly floats back towards the fisherman while naturals drift ignored over the trout's position—no rise, nothing.

Elsewhere on the river the fish continue their thumping rises but the two fish nearest the fisherman fail to show. The surface of the river looks like pink oil, reflecting the afterglow of the sunset. Not a breath of wind disturbs the slick surface, just the expanding rings of rising fish as they turn on the blue winged olives.

It is more than coincidence that only the fish nearest to the fisherman have stopped rising; some movement must have betrayed him. Once again it is time to think like a trout. Imagine what the surface of the water looks like from below. The whole underside must be like a shimmering pink mirror. The heavy shadows of overhanging trees have made the bottom of the stream darker. The only light that is penetrating is from that pink glow overhead. Now imagine what a floating leader, even a fine one, will look like on the surface of that mirror, the irregularities of the nylon dimpling the surface film.

Any of the irregularities remove the mirror-like polish of the surface, refracting in its place the shadowy colours of the bankside vegetation and overhanging trees. To the trout the outline of the trace must look like a large shadowy hawser that is attached to what looks like a natural fly. Few self-respecting trout will be tempted to snap at a fly so encumbered.

So what is the solution? Part of it can be wetting a few inches of the leader point so that it sinks without drowning the fly, and thus becomes far less visible. The first fish was probably put down by the angler's movements on the bank, so it is wise to stay as far back as possible, even if this means an uncomfortably long cast. Another solution can be to cast to the fish from right angles, while the angler keeps well back from the bank. This means that some of the line between the rod tip and the fish will land on the bank, rather than on the water, obviously bringing with it the risk of snagging the line or fly on the bankside undergrowth; but this risk is better than the certainty of putting down the fish. If the cast is accurate, no section of the trace will pass over the fish, only the fly, but drag may be a problem, so a slack line is better. I know of many fishermen who actually attach a thicker point in the evening, in the hope of taking a heavy fish, but I think it vital to fish as fine as possible.

Fortunately this period of ethereal light in the evening is relatively short-lived, and as the dusk deepens the fish become less sensitive and seem keener to take the fly. Even so, there is no point in wasting any opportunity that could provide a good fish, particularly as hatches of blue winged olive are notoriously brief.

A vital prerequisite for dry fly fishing is good eyesight. It is most important to be able to identify flies at some distance, to be able to see fish in the water, to be able to see rises and to tie knots in fine nylon in gloomy conditions. I have worn glasses for many years and, with advancing age, have found that I now need stronger lenses for close work. The solution to this problem used to be bi-focal and subsequently, where necessary, tri-focal lenses. Fortunately my deteriorating near vision coincided with the introduction of variable focus lenses. For those who are not familiar with these, they are made to your normal prescription but also have a graded magnifying capacity. As your eyes move downwards from looking some distance through the upper part of lens, the variable capacity of the lens gradually feeds in a stronger magnification towards the lower part.

For many years I have worn polarising prescription lenses for fishing, but these are not variable focus. Now I am confronted with a problem. Polarising lenses are not available, apparently, with variable focus, so it seems I may have to go back to wearing clip-ons which I find uncomfortable, cumbersome and far from satisfactory in terms of reflections and light transmission.

Having worn variable focus lenses for about four years, I can thoroughly recommend them. They are a real boon when fishing, because the grading of the lenses means that I can see good detail at considerable distances, while still being able to study a fly nearby on the water, or to look at my own artificial fly when held in the hand. I really cannot understand why it is that nobody is making polarising blanks for grinding variable focus lenses, but perhaps it is being investigated.

American fishing magazines offer a huge range of sight aids for fishermen, so perhaps it will not be all that long before someone over there comes up with a solution to my problem. What would really be ideal is a lens that has a progressive focus, is polarised and is light sensitive—that would meet all my needs—but for the time being I shall be happy if I can just find a polarising variable focus lens.

Those who are lucky enough not to have to wear prescription glasses should listen to just one warning. When buying polarising spectacles, make sure you test them thoroughly. A few years ago I bought some prescription polarising lenses that were quite unsatisfactory. The polarising section seemed to be only in the centre of the lens. When I looked through them they cut out a mere fraction of the refracted light and seemed to show a sort of star shape, with the centre polarising effectively, but with radial lines that expanded towards the edges of the lens, which were just the same as looking through a conventional lens.

When testing polarising glasses it is best to find a shiny surface and then put on the glasses to see how much of the shine is eliminated by the lenses. Move your head from side to side to check that the edges of the lenses work as efficiently as the centres. Having done that, roll your head to one side as if attempting to rest your ear on your shoulder. The best lenses are those that will tolerate the sharpest angle of view from that position before the shine reappears on the test surface. You may feel a bit of a fool standing in a shop rolling your head about, but you will have no regrets about choosing the best glasses once you are back beside the river.

In addition, remember to choose lenses with the minimum amount of tint, so that they are still useful in poor light. Nobody has yet been able to explain to me why polarising lenses must be tinted at all, but even polarising camera filters have some tint, so I can only assume that the tint is in the nature of the lens. When on a cross-Channel ferry recently I noticed some windows that were apparently polarised. They were made up of two sheets of glass, the inside one of which could be rotated. When this was done the window appeared to go black, exactly as happens when you rotate the lenses of two pairs of polarised sun glasses. These windows were absolutely clear when turned back to the transparent position, having no evidence of tint.

Chapter Four

The trout is a remarkably adaptable creature. He has had to tolerate man's interference with his environment for as long as people have taken an interest in rivers. In Chapter One I described how man shaped the chalk streams in order to make use of the surrounding land. What is interesting is how the trout has used this manipulation to its own advantage.

Almost any man-made object that interrupts or alters the flow of a stream becomes a lie for the trout. To be fair, the trout has always used irregularities in the general flow of water to its advantage, and the use of man-made objects is purely an extension of the fish's use of currents and eddies.

It is not surprising, therefore, that the weirs, bridges, culverts and sluices that proliferate on our rivers and streams become a magnet for the trout's attention, for here are safe lies that focus food into a small area and offer security from predators. For as long as man does not pollute the water flowing through these constructions, the trout is happy to take advantage of the situation.

To the fisherman these objects present an interesting problem, while generating great excitement because of their potential. There is no question that the largest fish in the water inhabit these areas; the best lies are always occupied by the biggest fish. Unfortunately, however, they are often difficult to fish. Old sluices, in particular, usually have nettles and brambles growing out of the walls, and you can guarantee that the best fish will be lying against a wall protected by a jungle of overhanging foliage.

This does not mean the fish is impossible to reach. A study of the flow patterns of the water will often reveal a place where the fly can be dropped so that the current will make it swing under the overhanging vegetation and over the nose of a waiting trout.

Those used to fishing in the clear and relatively calm waters of the open meadows may at first be daunted by the prospect of bridges, weirs and sluices, but it is worth noting that fish lying in these apparently unassailable conditions are usually far more approachable and far less fussy about the species of fly they swallow. Because the fish feels secure from predators, it is usually off its guard and is far less suspicious. It has little time to make a detailed study of the morsel it is being offered as it rushes by on the current. But while there are compensations for the difficulty in placing the fly, there are other problems to note. Rises in turbulent water are extremely hard to spot; the agitated state of the surface means that there are no visible telltale ripples to show where a fish has risen.

The first action, therefore, is to put yourself in the trout's position. Where is the best place to wait for food without expending too much energy on staying in position? Where is the fish least vulnerable from predators? Where is most of the food concentrated? If the fisherman can see a position in the water that offers a solution to these problems, it is virtually certain he will have located the lie of a trout.

Because rises are so difficult to identify, the next step is to sit and watch. Careful observation will reveal flies being carried through the sluice, past the wood and brickwork. Study the path of these flies minutely. Some will be seen to take off, others will be turned over by the current and struggle back to their feet, but some will disappear with no apparent explanation. Careful examination of this area will reveal the neb of a trout occasionally breaking the surface to intercept the spiralling flies in their headlong journey across the gully. Sometimes a movement that is out of place with the general pattern of the current will reveal a rising trout; on another you will be able to spot the waving tail of a fish that is not in synchronisation with the waving weed around it. Sometimes sunshine slanting down the brickwork or piling will cast a fish-shaped shadow.

Now is the time to devise a strategy—to work out the best place to drop your fly so that it will be intercepted by the waiting fish. Adrenalin is coursing through your blood—but stay calm! Weigh up all the facts and do not start casting until you are sure that you can cover the fish successfully. Go back to the basics. What fly is the fish taking? Where is the breeze coming from and how will it affect the landing position of the fly? How much room is there behind to allow for the back-cast?

Remember that once you start to cast you are committed. Although the fish is probably less on its guard than one lying in open water, it will be easily frightened if your fly catches in overhanging vegetation and has to be tugged free, and it could be alerted if you have to get to your feet in order to release a fly that is caught up behind you. So make sure that you are in the most comfortable and best possible position to place the artificial fly where it will be carried to the fish. Frequently in these circumstances you only get one chance, so make sure you are in a position to follow your fly along the current and see if it is intercepted by the fish.

There are other significant considerations. Once you have hooked the trout, how are you going to play it and where are you going to land it? If the sluice is simply a raised board with the water gushing under it, then everything must be done to prevent the hooked fish from charging through the gap and up into the water above. It is best to have a good look round before you start to cast. Frequently there will be a shingle or chalk bank sloping into the water downstream of the sluice, where a fish can be manoeuvred for netting out. If there are trees hanging low over the water, or dead branches have fallen in, these are obviously places to avoid.

As in any other case, the best time to steer a fish is immediately after hooking it. The trout is off balance and surprised, so do not give it time to gather its wits. Pull it downstream towards you, applying steady pressure, but remember to use the rod as a cushion to protect your vulnerable leader. Often space will be too restricted to play the fish with the rod held upright, so apply side-strain in the direction you want the fish to travel.

If your own movements are restricted, it is best to back out of your position as quickly as possible and pull the fish down into open water where your shingle bank can be used to help land the trout, or where there is an open bank which allows you to play it comfortably until it is time to net it out.

Because fish are less fussy about the flies they take in the security of sluices and weirs, it is possible to use more heavily dressed artificials than those that would be accepted out on open water. These have two main advantages—they are more easily visible on the tumbling water and they are more buoyant, being less vulnerable to drowning in the ripples and currents. The Skues pattern of little red sedge is an ideal fly to use in these circumstances. Sedges seem to frequent these turbulent areas and the trout are used to making a grab for them. If there are duns being washed down, then these obviously should be used, but they too can be dressed more bushily, with more body dubbing and a couple of extra turns of hackle. Those who do not tie their own flies should select the more generously dressed patterns at their tackle shop. Even commercially tied flies vary quite a bit in the amount of dressing on any given pattern.

While weirs and sluices can be dealt with in a similar manner, fishing under bridges requires a different technique because fish are very sensitive to movement at the bridge entrance, which is easily spotted from a darkened lie. The fisherman is at his most vulnerable as he enters the arch and is silhouetted against the bright background outside. It is necessary, therefore, to offer as small a profile as possible when passing through the bright arch and into the gloom. It is best to crawl along the bank, if there is one, or to stoop as close as possible to the surface when wading. If you are wading, remember to go slowly and gently. Do not allow your ripples to be washed upstream of you to alert the fish lying there.

Once you are actually in position, it is surprising how close you can get to rising fish. This is just as well, because head-room is usually restricted and a side cast or roll cast will often have to be used to propel the fly to the fish. Under these restricted circumstances it is difficult to cast delicately, but you must make sure that the fly alights gently—trout under bridges are very sensitive to surface movement.

In the face of these problems, however, there is a big compensation. Because of the light being transmitted through the water from the upstream side of the bridge, it is usually very easy to see fish in the water. Surface reflections are greatly reduced by the darkness overhead, so it is possible to pinpoint your fish accurately and to follow the progress of your fly on the surface. When fishing a nymph this offers a great advantage, for you will often be able to see your nymph in the water and to see the fish open and close its mouth when the nymph is taken. This is something that is often almost impossible to detect when fishing weirs and sluices.

Playing and landing fish under bridges is a different matter. If you want to catch more than one fish it is essential to get the hooked fish away from the others as quickly as possible, and with the least fuss. If you are wading it is usually not too difficult to back out, drawing the fish with you—but you risk betraying your presence to the others as you back through the lighted entrance.If you are fishing from a bank it is hard to control a fighting fish while trying to crawl backwards! It is a question of choosing the lesser of the evils that confront you—to remain where you are to fight the fish and allow the others to be scattered, or to risk losing the fish you have hooked while you fumble your way backwards into the open. I would usually opt for the backward crawl, if only because the limited head-room under most bridges makes it impossible to lift your rod tip high enough to draw the fish towards you when it is played out and waiting to be netted.

A word of warning about fishing under bridges or in weirs and sluices. Remember to check your hook regularly, particularly if you have seen your fly bounce off brickwork while you are casting. I remember rising a fish three times in fairly quick succession, but failing to hook it each time. I eventually looked at the hook and found that it had broken at the bend. This has happened to me several times since and seems to be a fairly common phenomenon. The force with which a hook is smacked into the brickwork during casting is obviously greater than one would assume.

I mentioned that I served my early dry fly fishing apprenticeship on the main river and carriers of the Hampshire Avon in the New Forest. All these carriers had their own sluices and one in particular stands out in my memory.

The carrier itself was one of the smaller ones, and although it was quite deep, it was very narrow. The two brick sides of the sluice were no more than three feet apart and they were draped with the inevitable brambles and nettles that tumbled over from the top and trailed in the water. The stream welled up from under a board that was semi-submerged.

I had always dismissed this particular sluice as being too small to hold any decent-sized fish, but on one occasion I was looking upstream at it when I saw a rise in the narrow area of clear water in the centre. The light in the sluice was too shadowy to be able to make out the size of the fish, but I decided that it was worth trying. It was quite impossible, because of the overhanging vegetation, to cast from anywhere other than straight downstream, which meant wading.

Because of the depth of the stream—the bottom shelved downwards towards the sluice—I could not get as close as I would have liked and therefore had to stand quite well back, with the water lapping just an inch or so from the tops of my waders. I waited for the fish to rise again and when it did I started false casting to work out line to cover it. There had been a few medium olives hatching elsewhere on the water and I had on my favourite fly at the time, a small Greenwell.

I shan't bore you with the number of times I was caught up in the overhanging foliage before I managed to land the fly in the small clear patch of water. Up came the trout and I hooked it firmly. It leapt out of the water, and it was huge! It plunged back into the sluice and went straight up under the semi-submerged board. I was powerless to stop the fish in its headlong rush and as the leader snagged the board, there was a snap. My line flew back and landed in coils around me. That, I thought, was that! The fish was gone and I wound in the line and went off in pursuit of other fish elsewhere.

It was a week later that I was back in the same place. I decided to climb into the stream and have a chuck up into the sluice in case another fish was there. I eventually landed my fly in the right area and once again there was a rise. I tightened and the fish leapt out of the water. I am sure it was the same fish. As it fell back I gave the line a hard, steady pull to try and turn the fish away from its emergency exit under the board. I felt the fish turn and then the line went slack. I reeled in. My fly was still there. The hook had obviously pulled free, but when I examined it more carefully I saw that it had been pulled nearly straight.

This sluice and this fish now became my priority. I walked there as soon as I arrived the following week. Again I rose the trout, and this time I attempted to turn it more gently. It worked! The trout shot downstream towards me. I was powerless to do anything. I couldn't recover line fast enough to keep up with the fish's hurtling dash. I thought that once it saw me in the water, effectively blocking its path in the narrow stream, it would turn and run back up towards the sluice. I should have known better. The fish shot straight past me, my line was caught round my waders and there was another 'snap!' as the leader parted and my protagonist swam to freedom.

My next visit to the sluice was a disappointment. Although I covered the lie several times there was no rise, and it was with a heavy heart that I scrambled from the water, up the steep bank and made my way to another carrier and, hopefully, another fish.

That should have been the end of the story. For two more weeks I put a hopeful fly over that tiny patch of open water, without response. I did not bother to go straight to the sluice the week after that, but when walking up in the evening I decided to give it one more try. This time I was fishing a sedge and eventually it landed just right. There was an eruption in the gloom. I turned the fish away from the sluice and, while holding it firmly with one hand, I scrambled up the bank before it could make its downstream rush.

The fish came past me as I cleared the water. It was towing a belly of slack line behind it and I was sure this would snag on some bankside protrusion before I could recover my line and my composure. Reeling in frantically, I set off in hot pursuit. At last I was back in control and the carrier opened out into a wider gravelly pool where I could play the fish with a degree of decorum. Eventually it came to my net. I could see the places in its jaw formerly occupied by my two flies, lost in our previous engagements. I hadn't the heart to kill the fish. I released my fly from its jaw and watched it as it flicked its tail and disappeared. I don't know how much it weighed, but it was by far the biggest wild trout I had caught to date.

This experience taught me that a trout that has a good feeding lie will not give it up lightly. Of course, there was no real proof that each confrontation was with the same fish, but the marks in its jaw looked as though they had been made by my lost flies. The period when I could not rise the fish in the sluice seemed to indicate that it was sufficiently intimidated to stay away for a while, but I suspected that what seemed a perfect lie was too good to give up permanently. What is interesting is that I never fished that sluice again, and although I couldn't resist an occasional peek, I never again saw a fish rise there.

Altogether there were five sluices on the Avon carriers and each had its own character. This was not a water that was netted or electro-fished, so there was a selection of coarse as well as game fish.

The first sluice controlling the flow out of the main river, which eventually fed all the other carriers, was a huge affair. It had two large gates, each about six feet wide, which fed the water into its brick-lined chamber. The trees above arched across, making overhead casting impossible. The only fishable bank was the one on the left, when looking upstream. For me, as a left-hander, it required a back-hand cast to get the fly up towards the fish that rose regularly in the turbulent chamber pool.

I spent many absorbing hours casting to these fish with an assort-ment of flies. The generally agitated state of the water, with its multiplicity of currents, made it difficult to keep a fly afloat and also to allow the fly to swim down on the current looking natural and without drag. I noticed that the fish in this sluice rose indis-criminately to any fly that appeared on the surface. These were not the fussy feeders of the open water—they had to grab any food that was available, or lose it to the torrent.

I had not at this stage learned to tie my own flies, but I gradually selected bushier patterns from tackle dealers' displays, specifically for use in the sluices. These flies floated longer and rode higher on the surface, with less tendency to drag. I fished patterns that no self-respecting smooth-water fish would have looked at, but their sluice cousins had to snatch first and ask questions afterwards. The sedge patterns, with their palmered bodies, became my favourites. Because of their gloomy character, sluices seem to be attractive to sedges, so there were usually naturals to be found in them at most times of day. Added to this, the indiscriminate habits of the residents meant that a well-placed sedge would often rise a good fish.

Since learning to tie my own flies I have gradually built up a selection of patterns that I use for sluices and bridges exclusively. They are generally larger and constructed on meatier hooks than I would normally use, since hooks are particularly vulnerable to encounters with timber and brickwork, losing their keenness and durability. A stronger leader point is also possible, since the agitation of the water surface allows a relatively coarse point to be used without detection by the fish. A strong point is a distinct advantage when you are repeatedly caught up on the weeds and broken timber that abound in these places.

The next sluice downstream of the main one was a fascinating affair. It had three distinct sections which provided ideal lies for fish. Upstream of it there was a deep pool that had been scoured by the water rushing under the gates. Fish lay on either side of this pool, taking advantage of the cover provided by overhanging bankside vegetation. A light scum built up on the surface where the water was temporarily slowed by the face of the gates. Several species of fly were caught in this film and large opportunist trout could duck out of hides to snatch the trapped insects.

It was this pool that was to provide me with the biggest native trout I ever caught at this fishery. I had occasionally glimpsed this fish as it plucked flies from the scum. During a good hatch of fly it would move out into relatively open water and take up station in front of a large ranunculus plant. Even in this open water it was not an easy cast. A fence and a gate were in such a position that standing in front of them put the fisherman in full view of the trout, and both were too high to be cast over in confidence.

I decided that the best position to cast from was therefore several yards back from the carrier bank, in a kneeling position in the field that was flanked by the fence. I took up my place almost opposite the fish, as far downstream as I could get without risking the back-cast being snagged in the fence. There was a steady trickle of mayfly floating down on the surface and I sat back on my heels to watch the trout as it rose to perhaps one in five of the flies that passed over it.

The style of the rise was that of a confident fish. It would pick out the fly it wanted and would slowly ascend to intercept the chosen insect. After taking the fly it would languidly wave its tail and drop back in the current to resume its post in front of the weed. I noticed that it only took the flies that were actually struggling on the surface. Those floating down inert were not intercepted. This posed a problem, because it is impossible to breathe life into a concoction of feathers bound down on a fish hook!

There was a stiffish breeze blowing upstream, and I eventually selected a mayfly pattern that was tied with broad wings of duck feathers—the wings were much more pronounced than in my other patterns and with any luck they would be twitched by the breeze as they passed over the trout's lie. It took just two casts to get the fly to the fish exactly right. I could clearly see the breeze twitching the fly as it floated down towards the fish. He came up and took the fly with complete confidence, and as his head went down I set the hook.

The trout gave a good strong fight, but was eventually subdued and in the net. He weighed three pounds fourteen ounces and was in outstanding condition. The pectoral fins were more than two inches long and his tail, when spread, must have measured more than four and a half inches across. Apart from being the largest, he was the most beautiful fish I had ever caught.

I was particularly proud of this fish. I had taken the time to watch its behaviour. I had overcome a number of difficulties and by a process of deduction had worked out the best way to persuade it to take the fly. In my experience it is rare to get everything right and be rewarded so handsomely for it.

Where the water ran under the sluice gates it was carried under a farm track by a wide brick culvert. This culvert was little more than eighteen inches above the water surface and held several good fish. Because of its height above the water it was difficult to cast up under the arch, but occasionally, if there was a strong southerly breeze, the wind would carry an artificial fly a few feet up inside the tunnel. The fish that lay in there seemed to mill around quite a bit and would sometimes drop back far enough to allow them to be covered by a wind-assisted cast. I caught several good trout from this place—but I never managed to hook one of the really big ones that could occasionally be glimpsed as they turned in the shadowy water of the tunnel.

Below the culvert was a deep and wide pool. This was inhabited by both trout and chub and it kept me absorbed for hours. The rate of flow through the pool varied according to the time of year and the adjustments made to the huge gates on the sluice controlling flow from the main river. There were more chub in the pool when the water was slacker, and it was sometimes difficult to tell, because of the huge beds of ranunculus, which species had taken my fly. The eddies and currents caused by the weedbeds, and the flow of water welling up after tumbling through the culvert, made the pool difficult to fish without drag and the trout, in particular, were fussy over patterns.

Downstream of this pool was a long, glassy glide as the water spread out and ran over golden gravel that was striped with trailing ranunculus. Below was a slower, slightly deeper run that led to yet another sluice. Above this sluice the carrier divided. The water that failed to plunge through the sluice gate made a right-angled turn to form another stream which ran across the easterly limits of the water meadows.

This sluice was guarded by a huge oak tree whose branches spread right across the top of the chamber walls. I mentioned in Chapter One that each sluice had its resident giant, and this one was no exception. The pool, scoured by the rush of water from the chamber, shelved steeply and the best way to fish was by wading. Casting was hampered both by the oak's overhanging branches and by the profusion of undergrowth that cascaded over the chamber walls and trailed in the water.

A cautious look through the tangle of vegetation revealed a trout of huge proportions lying against the far wall—partly camouflaged by fronds of trailing weed. Occasionally it put its nose outside its sanctuary to pluck a struggling fly from the surface or to intercept a nymph being swept past by the current.

The fish's lie was in relatively slack water where the current washed away from the chamber wall. The problem was to present a fly on the current so that it floated naturally down the torrent just beyond the fronds guarding the big fish. It was by no means easy because it was quite a long cast up into the chamber—the water was too deep to be able to wade close enough to make the cast comfortable.

In addition, the slack line that lay on the water between the fisherman and his quarry tended to be pulled to one side by the intervening current, causing the fly to drag away from its intended path.

On perhaps six occasions I persuaded the fly to run across the trout's lie in an acceptable fashion. Only once did the fish rise to the fly, but when I attempted to set the hook I felt a moment's resistance, and the fly then floated back towards me with no fish attached.

I spent many hours, over the three years I fished at the farm, trying to tempt this trout. I tried dry flies, nymphs, semi-sunken spinners, all with significant lack of success. It was one of those frustrating incidents which even now, nearly twenty years later, I still find perplexing. I can only assume that the problem was caused by drag which was undetectable from the distance of my casting position.

The rest of the sluice was by no means unproductive and I had many trout and grayling from it. It was the only place on the water where I caught grayling and, unlike the sluice upstream of it, I never saw a chub there.

I have already described my long-lasting battle with the fish on the small carrier on the eastern side of the farm water. There was one other small sluice that was also culverted. This was deep and narrow and the tunnel was no more than two feet in diameter, so there was no question of being able to get a fly more than a few inches inside it. On occasion, however, it was possible to see fish rise well inside the tunnel and I found it itchingly frustrating not be able to reach them. But I did learn a lesson as a result.

When the wind was favourable I made several efforts to get the breeze to help carry the fly a little farther up, but it always fell short of the nearest rise. The fish in this culvert behaved in a way similar to those in the other culverted sluice, in that I could sometimes see them jockeying for position. When this was going on they would sometimes mill round one another. It occurred to me that if I could place the fly in the entrance to the culvert at a time when a fish was facing the wrong way, it might possibly see it and give chase. I eventually got the timing right and a good-sized trout shot out of the tunnel entrance and grabbed my sedge.

I had to wait for the fish to begin to turn upstream before striking, but I caught it and it weighed just over two pounds. A few weeks later I took another fish in a similar manner.

My experience of fishing under bridges was very limited until I took a regular rod on the Itchen above Winchester. This fishery had one significant bridge that carried a major road over the main river, and there were two other bridges spanning one of the carriers.

At times when the rest of the fishery looked as dead as mutton, it was usually possible to find fish rising under the bridges. One of the carrier bridges presented a special challenge. It was probably no higher than four feet above the surface of the water and, when looking upstream, there was a bank to the right made up of concrete blocks to prevent erosion of the bridge foundations. These blocks were rounded at the edges but were uneven and uncomfortable to negotiate on hands and knees. To gain access to this bank the intrepid fisherman had to fight his way through tangled brambles, nettles and saplings.

It was the lure of fish which seemed to rise constantly beneath this bridge that forced me to endure the predacious undergrowth and the subsequent purgatory of the concrete blocks. The low roof of the bridge made an overhead cast out of the question. It was only possible to make a sideways twitch of the rod to propel the fly towards the rising fish. This was one occasion where I was grateful for being left-handed. At least my side-cast was clear over the water, but cobwebs hung from the low concrete ceiling of this gloomy place and frequently wrapped themselves round the fly as it grazed the underside of the bridge. If you think that a fly draped in cobwebs will float, you can forget it—it sinks like a stone! It was necessary, therefore, to keep the fly as low as possible while casting and to clean it regularly when it became wrapped in cobwebs.

These, then, were the problems that confronted me as I knelt on the concrete blocks under the bridge. The first time I ventured there two fish were rising. There had been several others, but they stopped as I struggled through the lighted entrance. Both the remaining fish were rising on the far side, one about four feet upstream of the other, and both relatively close to the upstream arch of the bridge.

I squatted as comfortably as I could while I contemplated the problem. My back was against the wall of the bridge, so there was no room behind me to extend line in order to cover the fish as they lay diagonally upstream of me. First of all I extended the line by casting directly upstream, and when I thought I had enough out to cover the nearest of the two fish, I switched the rod sideways so that it was parallel with the wall behind me. The forward cast propelled the fly across the stream, but it landed about six inches behind the rising fish.

Rather than extend any more line, I shuffled up another few inches and repeated the performance. The rod tip caught the bridge ceiling and the line landed in a heap. I started the procedure again and eventually covered the fish, which rose dutifully. I banged the rod against the bridge as I tried to tighten, but managed to twitch it sideways and set the hook. It was then that I realised I had given no thought to landing the fish. I could only use the rod to either side of me to control the bucking, plunging trout. Fortunately for me it ran upstream and I eventually managed to subdue it, playing it entirely from my left-hand side. It was not until I unclipped my net and extended the frame that I realised I had no way of pulling the fish over the net. Since I could not raise the rod tip, how on earth was I to pull the fish towards me without risking hand-lining it? Eventually I extended my rod arm sideways as far as I could, and as the exhausted fish was carried past me by the current I scooped the net under it and managed to draw it from the water. The other fish, which had been rising above the one I caught, took fright during the struggle and did not rise again.

I have related this experience in an attempt to illustrate why it is so important to think things through before casting. Had I made up my mind to back out from under the bridge as soon as I hooked the fish, I would not have put down the other one, which I suspect was larger, nor would I have risked losing the one I had hooked while I puzzled out a way to get it to the bank. It is not a conquest I am proud of—I was simply lucky.

Since then I have gradually improved my bridge-fishing technique. I have also realised that it is often better to go for the best fish first—even if this means putting down others that are downstream of it. If you want to take fish in sequence upstream of you it is necessary to employ a logic similar to that used in a game of chess.

It is vital to work out the strategy first and then modify your moves according to those made by your opponent but without losing sight of the original plan. At the same time it is essential to keep the hooked fish away from the others, and under a low bridge this means that you must back out where you can exercise full control, preferably on a short line.

Another bridge on the Itchen, which has also provided me with some good fishing, spans the main river. It was only possible to reach the left side of this bridge, when looking upstream. At some time in the past it had obviously been fished regularly, because it was equipped with a wooden walk-way piled into the river bed, which had long since fallen into disrepair. The water was deep below the walk-way, but fish rising upstream of the centre point of the bridge could only be reached from this vantage point.

I used to fish under this bridge with my friend, Bob Schröder, whose advancing years made him not all that steady on his feet. My heart used to be in my mouth as I watched him risk the questionable strength of the rotten timbers. Many of the planks were shattered or had gone completely, and the intrepid angler had to pick a wary route from one creaking supporting strut to the other in order to arrive at the best casting position.

Bob would stagger his way along this obstacle course, swaying and clutching at non-existent supports, his rod waving from one hand and his landing net frequently getting snagged on the rotten timber. How he failed to fall into the dark and troubled water below I shall never understand!

I mentioned earlier that once under a bridge it is rare for the fisherman to put down fish, except by clumsy wading or casting—but there is one interesting feature about fish that live under bridges. If they do suspect the presence of a fisherman they tend to continue rising, but they move upstream. Because the walk-way under the bridge was impassable beyond about the half-way point, it was necessary to make quite a long cast to reach those rising at the upstream end.

As I am predominantly a left-handed caster and it was necessary to fish with the right, I found it difficult to reach the farthest of the rises, so it was my duty to watch Bob as he cast to these fish at the extremity of range. What I learned from watching him was that the odd lighting under bridges tends to be transmitted through the water by reflections from the river bed and the silver underside of the surface. It is this feature which I think makes it difficult for the trout to see the fisherman, but it occurred to me that once the line and trace are floating on the water they must stand out like a snake where the light and shade penetrate the distorted surface film.

NM '90

Chapter Five

Surprisingly there are not all that many fly patterns that are needed by the dry fly fisherman, although the whole subject of water flies is a fascinating one and many fishermen become absorbed in it for its own sake, rather than just from a fishing aspect.

In Chapter One I discussed the flies that a beginner needs for his first season on the river. We all have our own favourite patterns, but the ten basic flies I listed form the back-bone of any chalk stream fisher's fly box. There are many fancy patterns which, in a way, serve to confuse the fisherman in his early days; I have found that over the years I have tended to discard many of those I used to carry and have instead replaced them with my own patterns which imitate the natural flies.

The fisherman who can tie his own flies has a distinct advantage over his fellows. He can style his flies to match exactly the size and colour of the naturals where he fishes. There is a quite remarkable difference in size and colour of the same species of fly on different rivers and even on different sections of the same river. Medium olives, in particular, vary quite markedly in size and colour according to the weather, the time of year and their location. If you tie your own flies it is possible to make patterns to cover every contingency.

A not inconsiderable advantage is also the difference in price. Once you have initially laid out the money to buy your fly-tying kit and a selection of cock feathers, you will find there is very little expenditure in topping up with materials as you use them.

This cost factor can have a significant influence on the way you fish. If you are having to pay out for shop flies you will often ignore fish lying in hazardous positions because you are worried about losing your fly. It is not only cost that causes this inhibition: people usually only buy three or four flies of the same pattern at any one time, so if they find one of these patterns is working particularly well on a given day, they will be loath to run short of that pattern by risking the loss of one on a fish lying in a position guarded by snags or bankside vegetation.

A further advantage is that you can tie flies on hooks of your own choosing. Some shop patterns are beautifully tied but are on hooks that are sometimes too heavy, too brittle or are inadequately tempered or sharpened. In some cases the materials used are inferior or the tying itself is fragile, so that the flies come undone the first time they are in contact with a trout's sharp tooth.

Don't misunderstand me—I am not saying that all commercially tied flies are bad. Most of them are beautifully tied with good materials, but they do restrict your options.

I began tying my own flies quite soon after I started fly fishing. In those days I had even less money than I have now, so it became an economic necessity. My bailiff friend was the first person I saw tying flies and I learned a great deal from watching him. He talked me into learning the art and I went out and bought a beginner's kit which was marketed at that time by Veniards, suppliers of all items for fly-tying.

In that kit was a selection of feathers, the basic tools needed, including a vice, various furs and some reels of silk. Also in the kit were two booklets, one containing a list of common fly patterns for trout and the other some very basic instructions. This second booklet was remarkable considering its size. I had no formal lessons in fly-tying and my bailiff friend only tied wet flies, which differ quite significantly in their tying technique—so I was on my own. It is a tribute to that little booklet that I learned to tie flies.

Needless to say, my first creations were appalling. There was no neatness about them. The hackle stood out at all angles, the body was knobbly, the tails stood out like a spray of flowers and the silk was discoloured from rubbing against my fingers. But eventually I tied a fly that caught a fish! To be fair I think it must have been a very unsophisticated and hungry fish, but it meant I was progressing.

I have known many people who have taken up fly-tying, and of these not many have persevered. Common excuses are that they have not had time, or they have the wrong sort of hands, or they are not good with their hands. This is nonsense. Unless a person is severely manually disabled, I am convinced that he can tie flies. Some people will be better than others, but I am sure that anyone, with sufficient perseverance, can tie a fly that is good enough to catch fish.

In my first chapter I said I did not believe that it was possible to learn to cast from a book, and I suppose that I should say the same about fly-tying, but as I learned the basics from a booklet, I have decided that it is worthwhile attempting to give a few fundamental instructions that may get you started. What I will say is that the easiest way to learn is to have lessons, preferably from a professional instructor, but if there are no classes near you perhaps a friend will have the patience to teach you. Failing both these options, there is a chance that this book contains sufficient advice to get you started.

First, therefore, it is necessary to list what you need, unless you buy a beginner's kit, as I did. I understand that there are some very good ones about nowadays, although buying the separate items yourself will probably be cheaper and you will not be lumbered with materials that you may never use.

The first thing you need is a vice. I prefer the sort with jaws that can be opened or closed with a simple knurled nut. I know plenty of tyers who prefer vices with jaws that are operated by a lever, but you must make up your own mind about this. You also need a good desk light—the universally adjustable type with a cup-shaped reflector is best. You need to be able to get the light as near as possible to the vice, but without impeding the movements of your hands around it, so the adjustable arm must be quite tall.

You need a good quality pair of embroidery or clinical scissors (the sort medics use for removing stitches are perfect). I have not yet found a thread better than Pearsall's Gossamer Silk. My advice is to avoid thread described as 'pre-waxed'. All the varieties I have tried are dreadful because they are sticky, come untwisted and snag during tying. Man-made fibres suffer from similar problems. To hold the silk you need a bobbin holder. The best sort has tapered spool holders which are sprung at each side to hold the reel. A central tube, through which the silk is fed, is attached to these springs.

At least two needles are required. One can be used to apply liquid wax for dubbing fur bodies, and the other is for applying varnish or teasing out trapped fibres. The needles are easier to use when equipped with handles.

It is possible to tie a whip-finish by hand, but a tool to help with this makes the job a lot easier. There is one made by Veniards which I know to be satisfactory, but my favourite came from Orvis of Stockbridge and is a much simpler device. Special pliers are made for winding in hackles and body materials. I find the teardrop pattern sold by Orvis the best.

The ideal knife to use is a surgeon's scalpel. Mine is made by Swan and Moreton and I bought it in a high street chemist's shop. The smallest variety commonly available is the best, and blades should be small and triangular, coming to a sharp point. You need some clear cellulose varnish. Clear nail varnish will do, but if you prefer you can buy fly-tyers' varnish from a tackle shop. If you are tying flies with dubbed fur bodies you will need some wax, which helps the fur to stick to the silk. The most satisfactory is a liquid called 'Flywax' and is available from tackle shops or mail order stores.

As for the consumable items, you need a number of cock capes. I have found that buying packets of cock hackle feathers is expensive and unsatisfactory. The colours you need to begin with should be limited to about six capes: Light ginger or light cree (mottled ginger); mid-brown/red; dark brown; light blue (which is really a light grey); iron blue (dark grey); and black. Other colours can be bought individually as your repertoire of patterns becomes more sophisticated.

It is possible to buy relatively cheap capes from most tackle shops and these usually come from India or China. A cock cape is taken from the back of the bird's head and neck, and ideally the feathers should have a good sheen. The individual fibres of each feather should stand out from the quill when bent and should not be soft and downy. When the cape is bent forwards the feathers should stand out from the skin and be springy. For dry flies most of the feathers needed are the small ones from the back of the bird's head, so capes with plenty of these smaller feathers are obviously better value for money than those with a short head and neck section. Individual capes can be bought for as little as £3, or it is possible to buy capes costing up to £60 which have been taken from birds specially farmed for the fly-tyer.

Many tackle shops keep a box of odd capes which are relatively cheap, and it is worth spending time sorting through in case there is a colour and quality that you particularly want. If I go into any tackle shop I always ask to look at their capes, just in case there is a treasure buried in the bottom of the box.

While I do make some flies with fur bodies, I have found that herl (individual large feather fibres) and quills make excellent dry fly bodies, so I would recommend that to begin with you only bother to buy a hare's mask (the whole of the face including the ears), and a mole skin. The effect of these furs cannot satisfactorily be substituted by herl in one or two specific patterns. You can go through oddments of knitting wool for various colours that might be suitable for dubbing fur bodies. Collecting pet hair of different colours can be quite amusing; some of my friends dread me turning up at their house clutching a pair of scissors and asking after their cat. My own dog sometimes gives me an old-fashioned look when I am sitting at my fly-tying bench! We used to have a lilac-point Siamese cat which had wonderful blue-grey areas of fur, and my wife told me she could not let the cat out after some of my snipping because the neighbours would think it was suffering from some appalling skin disease.

I tie virtually all my flies with wire ribbing on the bodies. This makes them far less susceptible to damage and coming undone. The best ribbing is fine brass wire, which is available from tackle shops, but it should be as fine as possible. The reel I use came from Veniards and measures just .005 inches thick.

When it comes to winging flies, most tyers use slips of feather cut from the primary wing feathers of various birds, but I prefer to use hackle point wings—normally used by most tyers only for spent spinners. I have found that feather-slip wings soon become damaged and lose their shape, but hackle points are easier to tie in and are much more durable. I would suggest the beginner should tie flies without wings to start with. These are called 'hackled' flies, and nearly all the standard patterns can be tied with or without wings.

It is worth spending a little time discussing the relative merits of winged flies compared with those that are simply hackled. Much research has been done on the subject and most conclusions seem to indicate that wings offer a trout its first indication that an object floating on the surface of the water could be a fly, and that the fish is therefore prepared to intercept it before the legs or body of the fly come into view.

Others argue that a hackled fly is just as convincing as a winged one and that the most important feature of a fly is the pattern that the hackles make in the surface film of the water. If that pattern is similar to the one made by the legs of a natural fly, then other considerations, such as wings, colour or size, are less relevant.

In my view the most important feature of any fly is the confidence with which it is fished. If the angler has confidence in his fly, he will normally present it better to the fish. In order to have confidence, the pattern must obviously comply with the fisherman's own observation of all that is happening on the water. The fly fished with confidence is therefore usually the right pattern for the circumstances pertaining at the time.

One of the features that gives me confidence in a fly is wings. If the fly sits up on the surface of the water and looks similar, from my point of view, to the naturals which are being taken by trout, then it should catch a fish. Therefore I tie all my dry flies with wings. You will notice that I specifically mentioned 'my point of view'. Nobody knows if a trout sees in a way similar to ourselves. I prefer to think that it does, otherwise our inadequate confections of fur and feather would not catch fish as often as they do.

It is important to remember that it is impossible to imitate a natural fly perfectly. Quite apart from the limitations imposed by the materials that go into an artificial fly's make-up, the whole thing has to be bound onto a hook, the point of which must be open and unrestricted by the dressing in order to hook the fish when it takes the fly. I have yet to see a natural fly with a built-in fish hook!

I regard the design of a fly rather like an impressionist painting. It can never be an accurate copy of the natural, so it is vital that it should be an accurate *suggestion* of the insect. It should be of a similar colour, size and shape and must suggest a living creature to the trout. The feathers and other materials should have a certain sparkle and translucence about them in order to suggest life and movement, and must otherwise comply with the features of the natural. If these conditions are followed, then the fly will normally catch fish.

Now that you have bought your fly-tying kit and set up your vice, the first thing to do is to put a hook in the vice. The hook should be set sufficiently far back in the jaws for the point to be shrouded, otherwise while tying you will tend to snag the silk on the hook point, with the risk of cutting or fraying it while you are tying. The hook should be held as firmly as possible by the vice jaws. Any movement while you are tying could be disastrous. Many vices have a rubber button on the base, which can be used to trap the silk while you are winding in other body materials. You also need another button or hook on your fly-tying bench to the right of the vice (I am assuming you are right-handed. If, like me, you are left-handed, these instructions should be reversed). This second button will be used to hold the silk at an angle at the front of the hook while you are winding in materials that will need to be secured immediately behind the hook eye.

While discussing hooks it is worth having a brief look at the huge quantity and range that are available. Probably the best for general fly-tying purposes are those made by Partridge of Redditch. What you want in a dry fly hook is something that is the right size, that is strong, light and sharp. There are some very good hooks made by Kamasan and I am very fond of a particular pattern by Mustad. Their hooks are smaller for a given size than most of the others and a Mustad 39849 No 14 is ideal for many of the general smaller dry fly patterns. These hooks also have a straight eye, rather than the usual pattern which is either cranked up or down. As a rule of thumb, if you prefer a cranked eye, up-eye hooks are normally used for dry flies and the down-eye for wet flies. I always used forged hooks. These have been hammered so that the sides of the bend are flat. This helps to prevent the hook from straightening when put under strain.

Having loaded your bobbin holder with a reel of silk and having threaded the silk through the tube, you should begin winding the silk on to the hook shank from the eyed end, working your way towards the bend. In order to lock the silk when you begin tying, it is necessary to make the first two or three turns overlap the loose end of the silk (see Figure 1). Do not apply too much tension to the silk or it will snap. You will gradually develop a feel for the right tension; most beginners make the mistake of applying too much. Once you have locked the silk behind the eye, you should hold the loose end with your left hand upwards at an angle from the hook shank, retaining a little tension. If you do this you will find that each turn of the silk, as you bind it down, will be stacked neatly behind the previous turn to make a tidy binding. This binding should be carried down the hook to a point just before the hook shank turns into the bend. Let the bobbin holder retain the tension of the silk by hanging loose while you use your scalpel to trim off the loose end behind the final turn of the binding.

The first of the actual body materials to be added to the fly are the tails. You will see from the patterns I shall list later that the tails are often of a similar colour to the hackle. The tails, therefore, are usually taken from the 'spade' hackles on the base of the same cape you are using for the hackle. These spade hackles are long and wide

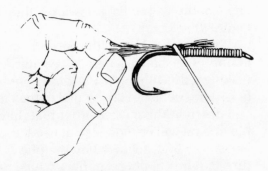

Figure 1. Lock the silk behind the eye of the hook before whipping down towards the bend.

Figure 2. Tie in the tails by lying them along the side of hook shank and allow them to be positioned by the silk tension.

compared with the feathers at the head-end of the cape. Pluck off an individual feather from the base of the cape and then pull a few fibres off the quill. These should not be the downy ones near the base of the quill, but should be as sharp and bright as possible, with plenty of 'spring' in them. As you tear off the fibres they will pull away together, attached by membrane. Leave this on the fibres as it will help to lock them together while you are binding them down on the hook shank, and can be trimmed off later.

There are two methods of tying in tails. You can pinch them between your finger and thumb with their thinnest end pointing to your left, away from the hook. You must hold them down, forcing them against the hook shank while you pull the silk down between your fingers and thus lashing them to the hook. Alternatively, while holding the thin end of the tail fibres in your left hand, you can form a coil of silk round the outside of them and the hook, with your right hand. As you pull t .s loose coil tight, the fibres will be lashed down at the tail of the body whipping. I prefer this method because it allows you to place the tails more accurately. You will find it best to hold the fibres to one side of the hook, so that as the coil tightens the fibres will be pulled on to the top of the hook. This action also helps to splay out the fibres in a flat fan, which will give the fly stability when it is floating on the water. Do not release the tension on the silk, but add another two turns of silk to complete the tying-in process for the tails. These additional two turns should be made neatly against one another, spiralling towards the eyed end of the hook (see Figure 2).

While still working at the tail end of the fly, now is the time to bind in any other body materials you need. Let us assume that we are making a fly with a pheasant tail fibre body, which is also to have a brass wire ribbing. Having tied in the tails, the other items should be tied down in the reverse order that they will be needed. In this case the ribbing will be the last item needed, so tie in about three inches of brass wire first, followed by the pheasant fibre. I usually use about three strands of pheasant fibre which have been snipped from close to the quill with a pair of scissors. For tying in the body materials you can use the same method that you used to tie in the tails.

I tie in my pheasant fibre with the thinnest ends bound down on the hook. This means that the taper of the fibres builds a thicker body towards the eye end of the hook, giving the fly a natural tapering shape. In order to make the fly as hard-wearing as possible, I trim the loose ends off immediately behind the hook eye. This means that the whipping silk overlays the body materials for the whole length of the hook shank, thus preventing them from being pulled out easily, as they would be if they were only secured by a few of turns of silk (see Figure 3).

Although I prefer winged flies, I think it would be less confusing if I simply described the construction of a hackled fly to begin with. I shall describe the winging process later, which you may like to adopt once you have mastered the initial skills.

You have now made a neat binding all the way back up to the eye of the hook. This layer of silk holds down the trimmed ends of the body materials, so that they are no longer visible. Release some more silk from the bobbin holder as that you can fasten the thread under the button on your fly-tying bench. The strand of silk should now extend forwards and downwards from immediately behind the hook eye, and be held under firm tension by the button on the bench. If the pheasant tail fibres are long enough, use your thumb and index finger to wind them in. If they are too short to manage in your fingers, the fibres can be gripped with your hackle pliers—but I prefer to use

Figure 3. Tie in the pheasant tail fibre and brass wire and then whip back along the hook shank to the eye.

Figure 4. Having formed the body, tie in the hackle stalk with three turns of silk, then make a few turns behind the hackle.

my fingers if I can because they have the advantage of sensitivity. The fibres should be wound down on the hook in a parallel spiral so that they do not overlap each other, but are sufficiently tightly wound in together completely to cover the silk binding beneath them. When the fibres have been wound in to within one turn of the eye, release the tying silk from the button and, while retaining the tension on the fibres to prevent them from uncoiling, trap them with three turns of silk. The thread can now be replaced under the bench button and you can use your scalpel to trim off the unused length of fibres, as close to the hook as possible. Be very careful when you do this. It is very easy to cut the silk while trimming the body materials.

In order to finish the body it is now ˙ ᴉcessary to make some open coils of brass wire that will give the body a segmented appearance, like the body of a natural fly. Keeping plenty of tension on the wire, wind it in an open spiral up to the eye. Make each coil roughly the same distance apart to retain the body's neat appearance, although you can make the coils at the tail end closer together than those nearer the hook eye. This imitates quite accurately the tapering segments of the natural fly's body. Finish your last coil a short distance from the eye and release your silk to bind the wire down in the same way as you did for the pheasant fibre. Finally, twist the wire until it breaks off where it has been trapped by the silk. That is the body completed.

The only other job remaining is to tie in the hackle. When selecting the right size of hackle for the particular hook size you are using, tease out one feather from near the head end of the cape and bend the quill. The individual feather fibres will then stand out in an arc. The feather you want should have about one and a half times the depth of fibre as the gap between the hook point and the shank (called the hook's 'Gape'). Pluck a suitable feather from the cape and, trapping the quill-end at the bottom of the feather between your index finger and thumb nail, scrape off all the soft and downy flue running up from the base of the quill, leaving the hackle stalk bare to the point where the shiny, springier fibres of the feather start. The better quality the hackle, the less will have to be trimmed from the bottom of it.

Holding the feather (with the base of the quill pointing down-wards) against the hook shank with your left hand, just behind the eye, use the silk to bind the quill to the hook. The binding should be on the clear section of quill immediately below the point where the fibres sprout from it. Having bound down the stalk with three firmly-tensioned turns of silk, trim off the excess bared stalk and then bend the fibrous part of the feather towards the eye so that you can put another three or four turns of silk in a coil to the left of the hackle without trapping the fibres (see Figure 4). Secure your silk under the button on the base of the vice. Using the hackle pliers, grip the top (smallest) fibres of the hackle and quill together, and wind in three or four parallel turns of hackle, so that the fibres stick out at right angles to the hook like a chimney sweep's brush. Still retaining the tension (not too much) on the hackle to prevent it from coming uncoiled, release your silk and bind down the last coil of hackle quill with a couple of turns. Now, keeping steady tension on the silk, wind it through the hackle fibres, back to the eye of the hook. Leave your hackle pliers clipped on to the dangling unused portion of hackle until you have completed this manoeuvre. While applying tension to the hackle pliers, use the scalpel to trim off the unused portion of the feather, as close as possible to the hook shank, but be careful not to cut the silk or the body materials (see Figure 5).

The last job is to complete the fly's head with a whip-finish. When you bought a whip-finish tool it came with instructions. Basically,

Figure 5. Using hackle pliers, wind in several turns of hackle before securing the end, and then wind the silk through the splayed fibres, back to the hook eye.

Figure 6. The finished hackled fly, after the whip finish has been completed and the silk trimmed off. A small drop of varnish will make sure it does not slip.

what you are doing is overlaying the loose end of the silk thread with several loops. When these are pulled tight the loose end is trapped and can be trimmed off without the fly coming unravelled. Using your dubbing needle, get a drop of cellulose varnish on the point and apply it to the whip finish to prevent it from slipping. You have just tied your first fly! (See Figure 6.)

If you want to tie a fly with a fur body, the fur needs to be spun on to a length of silk so that it can then be wrapped round the body and is trapped by the silk. Use your dubbing needle to collect a small quantity of liquid wax on the point. Rub the wax into a short length of the silk. Having selected your fur and trimmed it so that it forms a manageable bunch, grip it between your right thumb and index finger. Apply it to the waxed length of silk, rolling it between your thumb and finger so that it is spun on the silk.

Only experience can tell you how much fur you need for a given pattern, but on most flies you will probably only need to coat about an inch and a half of silk in order to whip it down a size 14 hook shank. If you have spun too great a length of fur on to the silk, you can slide it down the silk using your thumb nail and then pick it off once you have slipped it far enough to be clear of the waxed section.

What I suggest you do to begin with is just to practise on one pattern until you think you have made a fairly competent job of it. Do not get discouraged when it all goes wrong, as it inevitably will. If you persevere you will suddenly find that it all comes together and you will wonder how you ever found it so difficult. If just one part of the process goes wrong, do not unravel the whole fly; only unwind to the point where you made the mistake and carry on from there. As with most other jobs, fly-tying is greatly helped by good tools, so get a decent vice and the best scissors, hackle pliers and whip-finish tool that you can afford.

I warned you earlier that I prefer winged dry flies and that once the tying of the simple form of hackled dry fly had been mastered it was worth learning how to tie winged flies. The advantage of using hackle point wings has already been described. While feather slips may look more like the classic chalk stream flies, they are difficult to tie and easily damaged. It is impossible even to dry a feather slip winged fly without making the individual wing fibres separate and look all tatty.

Hackle point wings may be used in two modes: they can be set at right angles to the hook shank to imitate a spent spinner; or they can be pulled up into a vertical 'V' shape in order to represent a dun floating on the water, waiting for its wings fully to unfurl and dry.

The initial method of tying in both forms of wing is the same. If you study the previous section on tying a hackled fly, it is divided into two main manoeuvres—tying the body and tails and then tying in the hackle. To tie a winged fly you make your fly body as already described. When you have ribbed the body with the brass wire, you then take the silk back towards the bend, giving it just two or three turns down the shank, to leave sufficient space between that position and the eye to accommodate the wings and subsequently the hackle.

I described earlier how the spade feathers on a given cape could be used to make the tails and how the smaller head and neck feathers were used for the hackle that imitates the fly's legs. This leaves a large central section of the cape which is generally unsuitable for either purpose. One of the things that appeals to me about hackle point wings is that they use this central section of the cape, which is useless for any other purpose when making dry flies—apart, perhaps, from mayflies or other very large patterns.

These feathers are ideal for winging, but not from capes of all colours. An analysis of the wing colour descriptions given in the *Dictionary of Trout Flies* or *Trout Fly Recognition* will show that most of the Ephemeridae have wings of varying shades of blue (grey). As you build up your selection of capes it is worth keeping an eye open for any capes in these shades. The quality of the cape does not matter too much for wings, although they need to be reasonably stiff and springy if they are to hold their position once they are attached to the fly. If they are too downy they will tend to become waterlogged while fishing.

As spinner wings are simpler to tie than duns, I shall begin with a description of how I tie these. Most spinner wings are imitated with very pale blue, or even white, feathers. Depending on the pattern you are making, choose the correctly coloured cape and then go through the central feathers that match in size, shape and colour. It is surprising, particularly with dyed capes, how the colour varies from feather to feather.

When you have found a matching pair, pluck them from the skin.

To prepare the feather, strip the flue from the quill, leaving just enough of the feather fibre on the quill to give the correct length of wing. Wing lengths vary according to the pattern of fly. When you have prepared the feathers, arrange them between the thumb and index finger of your left hand, with one feather laid across the top of the other and the tips pointing in opposite directions (see Figure 7). Now lay the two feathers along the top of the hook shank and form a loop of silk round them and the hook, with the loop in the position on the fly body where you want the wings to sit. As you start to tighten the loop, turn the feathers so that they stand out at right angles on top of the hook, like aircraft wings.

Pull the silk relatively tight, but not completely so. Because you have turned the feathers while tightening the silk, you will see that the thread forms a diagonal line dissecting the centre of the wings. While still holding the wing feathers with the left hand, pass the silk round the underside of the hook shank and bring it across in the opposite direction so that the silk has now formed an 'X' pattern on top of the wings. Repeat this three times—effectively making a figure

Figure 7. For a winged fly, select two suitably sized hackles and, after plucking off the excess flue, place them in your fingers so that they point in opposite directions.

Figure 8. Bind the wings down on the hook shank using a figure-of-eight knot, so that the feathers stand out at right angles to the hook.

of eight over the top of the wings and the underside of the hook shank. If the feathers slip in your fingers while you are doing this, pull them back into the right position while allowing the silk to slacken just enough to complete the action (see Figure 8).

Give the silk one more turn round the hook shank, just in front of your figure-of-eight fastening, and leave the bobbin hanging by its own weight to retain tension on the thread. Using one hand for each feather, pull each quill by its root GENTLY so that just the tips, which have the fibre remaining, are left projecting on either side of the shank (see Figure 9). While retaining tension on the bobbin, make another two figures of eight round the wing roots and then make another turn of silk round the hook shank, between the wings and the eye. You are now left with a large overhang of unwanted quill on

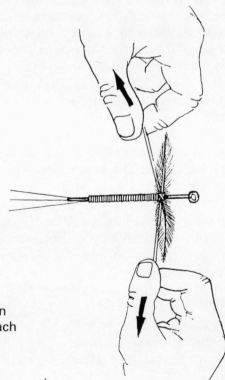

Figure 9. While using the bobbin holder to tension the silk, pull each of the hackle stalks through the knot so that the wings are of correct and equal length.

each side. Using your thumb and index finger, gently pull these quills forwards towards the eye of the hook so that they lie on either side of, and parallel to, the hook shank. While retaining gentle tension on the quills, make another two turns of silk round them and the hook shank, so that they are held firmly. Now, release the bobbin to hang by its own weight, and trim off the remaining unwanted quill, then continue whipping back to the hook eye, ready for tying in the hackle.

Finally, to make sure the wings are secure (and before you tie in the hackle in front of the wings) take a droplet of varnish on your dubbing needle and apply it to the figure-of-eight knots that are securing the bases of each wing.

It is obviously important that you tie in the wings sufficiently far from the eye of the hook to allow room to wind in the hackle and to allow sufficient space for the whip-finish. Some tyers prefer their hackle wound both in front of and behind the wings. If you prefer this method it is simply a question of giving two turns of the hackle in front of the wings, and then carefully feeding it past the wings to allow for another two turns behind them. If you do this, however, remember that after tying in the root of the hackle you will have to take the silk back to a position behind the wings in order to tie down and secure what is, effectively, the fourth turn of the quill.

If you wish to pull the wings up into the dun position, you secure the wings as described for the spinner, but instead of whipping the silk back up to the eye, ready for the hackle, you leave the bobbin dangling just in front of the wings. Taking your thumb and index finger under the hook, you squeeze both the wings so that they are bent up into the familiar 'V' shape of the dun. You then carefully run the silk round the outside of the base of both feathers, applying just enough tension to pull the wings upwards and hold them in the desired position. It may be necessary to make two of these turns round the wing roots in order to get them pulled up at the correct angle (see Figure 10). When the angle has been achieved, you retain the tension while making a further pass with the silk round the hook shank in front of the wings. Then make a further figure of eight across the wing roots, so that the loop round the wings is locked in position and cannot slip or come undone later. The procedure for tying in the

Figure 10. After pushing the wings up into a V-shape with your fingers, form a loop of silk round the base of the wings to hold them in the upright position, then secure this loop with a figure-of-eight knot and a drop of varnish.

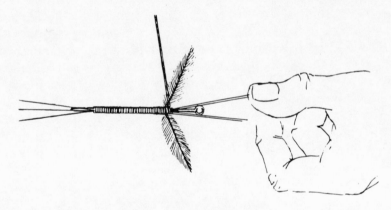

Figure 11. Pull the two hackle stalks forward and bind them down with several turns of silk before trimming them off.

Figure 12. The finished winged fly after the hackle has been added.

unwanted quill ends is the same as for the spinner, but before tying in the hackle, remember to add the droplet of varnish to the wing roots for added security (see Figures 11 and 12).

Chapter Six

Having mastered the technique of tying your own flies, you will next have to choose the patterns that you want to tie. I have found over the years that although the orthodox patterns listed in a number of books may be an ideal starting point, you are likely to find that you either do not have the precise materials listed, or that the pattern does not accurately represent the fly as you have seen it where you fish. As you continue to tie your own flies you will find yourself modifying patterns for your own purposes. The flies I have listed in this chapter are all patterns I have tied and used myself and have found to be the best for my purposes.

Every species of fly varies quite significantly from one area to another, and even from one stretch of the same river to another. Flies like the medium olive and the large dark olive also vary in colour and size according to the time of year and prevailing temperatures. In the case of spinners, their body colour varies according to their age, so the flies seen on the bankside vegetation will often be quite a different colour from those that are lying dead on the surface and being eaten by trout.

Because spent spinners are obviously immobile, the trout normally take them in a leisurely manner; this means that they are subject to a closer scrutiny by fish than are duns since there is no risk of their escape. Both colour matching and size matching are therefore most important.

The easiest way I have found of catching water flies is with a cheap plastic tea strainer that has a fine mesh. This can be attached to the tip of your fishing rod with a few twists of a small elastic band. If you would rather not use your rod you can use the extended handle of your landing net, although this obviously gives less reach.

Large Dark Olive

The first ephemerid of the chalk stream fisherman's season is the large dark olive. It is a relatively slow-moving fly which needs some time on the surface after hatching before it can fly. On fisheries that begin the season in April, the large dark olive may well be the only fly on the water, and therefore can have an important role. The fly is a dirty olive-brown colour with mid blue-grey wings, and the male is often slightly darker than the female, although I use just one pattern to imitate both.

Hook: Partridge or Kamasan up-eye size 14.
Silk: Pearsall's dark olive.
Body: Dark browny-grey hen pheasant tail feather herl (three strands tied in parallel).
Rib: Fine brass wire.
Hackle: Dark speckled brown/black cock.
Wings: Mid blue-grey cock hackles tied in 'dun' position.
Tails: A small bunch of fibres taken from the spade feathers of the hackle cape.

It is obviously easiest if you can capture a large dark olive for yourself to see the exact body colour. Many large dark olives that are tied commercially have far too much green in them. Although the fly is often described as being an olive colour, to me it looks more a dark, muddy brown. The hen pheasant tail fibre I advocate for the body should have some darker stripes in it. When wound in this gives a good segmented effect and the overall colour of the body is just right. I recommend a speckled hackle feather because I happen to have one that is ideal, but any mid to dark brown hackle will do.

For the nymph of the large dark olive I use the dark fur from a hare's face with a rib of fine gold wire. An extra couple of turns of the body dubbing close behind the hook eye represents the thorax and wing cases.

This early in the season it is rare to get an evening rise, with the result that a spinner pattern for the large dark olive seems to have little use. I don't think I have ever noticed a rise to a large dark olive spinner. If you do want a spinner pattern I would recommend my pattern of pheasant tail spinner described for the medium olive, but tied on a size 14 hook.

GRANNOM

On some rivers there is a fly that can produce exceptional fishing during April and early May. This is a sedge—the grannom. The hatches are usually short-lived and general opinion is that the flies are taken more while they are just hatching than at any other time. I have fished hatches of grannom on both the Test and carriers of the Avon and have found them very frustrating. However, I have had some success on a few occasions with one particular pattern.

Hook: Mustad 39849 straight-eye size 14.
Silk: Pearsall's gossamer green.
Body: Mixed buff and black fur from a hare's ear.
Rib: Fine brass wire.
Hackle: Dark brown-red cock.

I have recommended green silk only because everyone else seems to use it. The adult female grannom carries a green egg sac under her tail when returning to the water to lay her eggs, but as my pattern is an attempt to imitate the hatching larva, the use of green silk really seems superfluous. However, as the pattern sometimes works I can see no point in changing the colour, although I suspect that dark brown would work just as well. The hook I have recommended is slightly smaller than most other manufacturers' size 14. It would probably equate to a standard size 15 if odd sizes were readily available, and it has a straight eye, which I prefer.

Medium Olive

The chalk stream fisherman owes more to the medium olive than to any other fly. Hatches begin in late April or early May and continue throughout the summer, extending to the end of the season. Medium olives early in the season are darker than those hatching in hot weather, and the early flies can sometimes be a little larger than their later cousins. Although flies like the iron blue and blue winged olive may promote more enthusiasm for a short time among chalk stream trout, it is the medium olive that offers the fish their daily bread. While hefty mayflies or scuttering sedges may tempt big trout that are not normally interested in taking flies, the average angler is more likely to catch more fish on a good pattern of medium olive than on any other species.

Hook: Mustad 39849 size 14.
Silk: Pearsall's gossamer olive.
Body: Olive dyed heron herl (where available) or dyed Canada goose wing primary herl.
Rib: Fine brass wire.
Hackle: Cree or ginger cock.
Wings: Mid to pale blue-grey hackle points tied in 'dun' position.
Tails: Small bunch of fibres taken from spade feather of the hackle cape.

If you look at the medium olive it is really quite a drab little fly. The overall impression is a mid to light-brown muddy colour, with just a touch of washy green. I am fortunate enough to own a number of heron feathers that are dyed the perfect colour to imitate the body of the medium olive. However, because of the ban on heron feathers, it is no longer possible to get these and I have found that a good alternative is to use individual fibres from the Canada goose primary wing feather.

These fibres are remarkably similar in shade to natural heron, although they contain more brown. Experiments by my friend Bob

Schröder have shown that the application of flavine (an old antiseptic containing a yellow dye) to the feathers turns them the muddy olive colour that is needed. In former days picric acid was used to get this colour, but the acid no longer seems to be available. You should be able to get one of the flavine antiseptics made up by your local chemist, but ask him for a strong solution (0.4 per cent). I just paint the area of feather to provide enough material needed at any one time for my medium olives. It dries very quickly and seems to be colour-fast, and it is proof against the carbon tetrachloride that is used in modern dry fly floatants. I have yet to see how the colouring withstands the test of time.

Gold Ribbed Hare's Ear
In my view the best imitation for the hatching medium olive nymph is the gold ribbed hare's ear. This can be tied in a variety of colours, and the fur need not only be taken from the ears. The classic pattern is with light-brown fur taken from the ears, which also contains a touch of black. The fly does not need to be winged, but the body should be tapered, with extra dubbing at the thorax. The fur at the front of the thorax should be teased out to represent straggly legs just emerging from the nymphal shuck. If fish are proving difficult to take on a dun, this pattern will nearly always provide the solution if fished in the surface film. It should be ribbed with fine brass wire.

For fish that are obviously taking nymphs below the surface during a hatch of medium olives (or at other times, too), I use a hare's fur pattern, but tied with the darkest fur taken from a hare's face, just between the ears. This fur contains a mixture of brown and black. The body is dubbed and ribbed as for the hare's ear, but no fibres are teased out and I trim the body with sharp scissors to give it a neat tapering shape all round. I fish this nymph wetted, so that it sinks an inch or two below the surface. It can be deadly for difficult fish that will look at no other artificial.

Pheasant Tail Spinner
Tied in various sizes, the pheasant tail spinner for me is the most useful spinner pattern in my fly box. It can be used to imitate spent large dark olives, medium olives, pale wateries, blue winged olives and female iron blues.

Hook:	Partridge or Kamasan size 14 (for large dark olive) or size 16 for the female iron blue. Use the size 14 Mustad hook for the medium olive.
Silk:	Pearsall's gossamer hot orange.
Body:	Deepest rusty-red cock pheasant tail fibres (three strands tied in parallel).
Rib:	Fine brass wire.
Hackle:	Dark red cock, just two turns are sufficient.
Wings:	Palest blue-grey cock hackle points tied 'spent'.
Tails:	A few strands of white cock hackle fibres.

IRON BLUE DUN

The iron blue dun is traditionally seen as the fly of blustery days in May and June, although it puts in sporadic appearances in August and sometimes September, too. For some reason, although a small fly, it is particularly attractive to trout. I suspect that its attraction is not so much its flavour as the activity it shows when hatching and its subsequent attempts to get airborne. Whatever the reason, iron blues seem to be singled out by the fish at times when several species of fly may be on the surface at the same time.

Hook:	Partridge or Kamasan up-eye size 16.
Silk:	Pearsall's gossamer claret.
Body:	Three strands of darkest undyed herl from primary wing feather of Canada goose.
Rib:	Fine brass wire.
Hackle:	Small dark blue-grey cock or ginger cock.
Wings:	Dark slaty blue-grey hackle points tied in 'dun' position.
Tails:	Small bunch from spade feathers of the hackle cape.

For some time I could not understand why several standard patterns advocated the choice of ginger cock hackles, iron blue or dark brown for the same fly. Although I had examined several natural iron blues, the colour of the flies' legs always looked dark blue-grey to me. John Goddard's *Trout Fly Recognition* came to my rescue. The legs on the male dun are described as being dark olive brown, but on the female as pale olive-brown. My own pattern, as above, uses an iron blue hackle which works very well for me.

If you wish to tie both male and female patterns, I suggest you stick to the iron blue hackle for the male, but use a ginger one for the female. The body colour also varies between the sexes, so if you want to be fussy, I suggest the recommended feather for the body material, but use the fibres nearer the thick end of the quill for the female, because these are paler.

I have already suggested the use of the pheasant tail spinner to imitate the spent iron blue female. Obviously, because she returns to the water to lay her eggs, the female spinner is found on the water in greater numbers than the male, but it may be worth carrying a pattern to imitate the male (sometimes called the Jenny spinner), because I have often seen them on the water.

Hook: Partridge or Kamasan up-eye size 16.
Silk: Pearsall's gossamer dark brown.
Body: Four turns of brown silk at the tip of the tail with the rest of the body tied with white floss.
Hackle: Mid-blue cock, just one or two turns.
Wings: Pale blue cock tied 'spent'.
Tails: Few strands of white cock hackle taken from a spade feather.

You will find, when you tie in the wings, that the dark brown silk gives the fly a dark thorax and head. When varnished this goes nearly black, which is ideal because the natural fly has similar colouring.

I find that my dark hare's ear nymph makes a very good representation of the iron blue nymph when tied on a size 16 hook.

SPURWINGS AND PALE WATERIES

For many years fishermen were led to believe that the spurwings and pale wateries could be treated as the same fly. In the case of the smaller spurwings this is probably still true, but the large spurwing is more like the colouring of the blue winged olive and it is worth tying a separate pattern for this.

For the small spurwings and pale wateries I had great difficulty finding a really good pattern until I came across the late Richard Walker's book *Fly Dressing Innovations*. He lists two patterns that I have tried and they both work better than anything I had previously concocted.

The first, called 'The Enigma', was devised by Pat Russell of Romsey and is very simple to tie.

Hook: Partridge or Kamasan up-eye size 16.
Silk: Pearsall's gossamer white.
Body: Cream cock hackle stalk.
Hackle: Best quality pale cream cock, tied very sparsely.
Tails: A small bunch of cream cock hackle fibres.

Pat Russell later modified this pattern, tying in the hackle the length of the hook, with the quill of the hackle forming the body, but I have found this version far less successful than the original.

Richard Walker's own pattern is:

Hook: Up-eye size 16.
Silk: Pearsall's gossamer primrose.
Body: Swan's wing secondary feather herl tinted pale greenish-grey with a few turns of tying silk exposed at the tail end.
Hackle: Deep cream or honey dun cock.
Wings: Palest blue cock hackles tied in 'dun' position.
Tails: A small bunch of honey dun or deep cream cock hackle fibres.

For the wings his pattern suggests a bunch of cream cock hackle fibres or the use of bleached starling feather slips, but I have substituted my own hackle point wings and they seem perfectly acceptable to trout. He also recommends a touch of cellulose varnish on the silk whippings at the head and tail of the fly body. This gives the silk a slight amber tint.

For the large spurwing I use the size 14 Mustad hook already mentioned. In order to make the fly look bigger I use a larger hackle than the one for the medium olive but of a similar colour. I also tie the body slightly fatter, using the dyed Canada goose feather, and I make the tails longer than for the medium olive. For the wings I use dark blue hackle points tied in the 'dun' position, which are larger and darker than those used for the medium olive.

Tying a larger fly on a small hook can be a useful dodge when imitating a fly of a particular size, where there is no correspondingly suitable size of hook. This principle can also be used in reverse, so that a small fly can be tied on a relatively large hook. This can be

ARTIFICIAL FLIES	NATURAL FLIES

Large dark olive	Large dark olive

Grannom	Grannom

Medium olive dun	Medium olive dun

Latex mayfly	Mayfly dun

ARTIFICIAL FLIES	**NATURAL FLIES**

Mayfly spinner

Mayfly spinner

Iron blue dun

Iron blue dun

Enigma

Pale watery dun

Hawthorn fly

Hawthorn fly

ARTIFICIAL FLIES	**NATURAL FLIES**

Black gnat

Black gnat

Jenny spinner

Jenny spinner

The author's orange quill

Blue winged olive dun

Pheasant tail spinner

Blue winged olive spinner

ARTIFICIAL FLIES	**NATURAL FLIES**

Little red sedge

Cinnamon sedge

Large dark sedge

Large brown sedge

NYMPH PATTERNS

Hare's fur nymph

Gold ribbed hare's ear

Artificial flies shown on the left have been arranged opposite their natural counterparts with the exception of the last two on this page, which are reproduced to show the different tying styles used for the two hare's fur patterns.

The photographic lighting and reproduction process have marginally lightened the colour of the wings on the artificial flies, so feathers a shade or two darker than the illustrations should be used for winging.

The photographs of natural flies were kindly supplied by Taff Price, with the exception of three: the medium olive dun which was kindly lent by John Goddard, and the iron blue dun and blue winged olive dun which were taken by Dave Tait. All the artificial flies were photographed by Peter Gathercole.

useful where you might be worried about the holding potential of a small hook, particularly when imitating tiny flies like caenis.

Mayfly

Being primarily an upper Itchen fisherman, my experience of mayfly fishing is limited compared with those who have regular rods on such rivers as the Kennet, the Avon and the Test. However, I had a number of seasons when I fished the Avon and part of the Test at Romsey, and for several years I had a regular date with a friend fishing mayfly on the Gloucestershire Coln at Fairford. My fishing experience with the mayfly now looks as though it is to be further expanded by the resurgence of that fly on the upper Itchen. The species has put in an ever growing presence on the river from early June and into July during the last three years. The resurgence is all the more remarkable because hatches on the upper Itchen have been unknown for the most of the twentieth century.

Quite why the fly should have reappeared I do not know, unless the hand of man has been at work and mayfly nymphs have been introduced from elsewhere. One other possible explanation could be the reduction in flow on the river as the result of ever-increasing abstraction by the water authority. This has led to deepening silt deposits, which favour the mayfly larvae. The mayfly can be regarded as a mixed blessing. There is no question that on rivers with big hatches the fish seem to stop rising to more mundane flies once the main mayfly hatches are over. I am not convinced by the argument that the trout become gorged on mayflies, but there is no question that there is a dearth of rising fish for some time afterwards—a lull that does not seem to occur on rivers without mayfly hatches.

Regardless of the pros and cons of mayflies, anyone who fishes a river where these flies are native cannot possibly ignore the opportunities offered. I must add that the old expression 'duffers' fortnight' when applied to the mayfly phenomenon is not true in my experience. Trout can be as fussy when taking mayflies as they are with any other fly, sometimes more so.

I fish two patterns of the mayfly dun. The first is my variation of the famous Irish 'Gouldon's Favourite'. The wings are optional.

Hook:	No 10 or 12 long shank (according to the size of the natural mayflies where you are fishing).
Silk:	Pearsall's gossamer brown.
Body:	Natural raffia, with a few turns of the base silk left exposed at the tail.
Rib:	Fine brass wire and dark brown tying silk.
Hackles:	1, rusty-red cock; 2, hot orange cock; 3, cree or light ginger cock.
Wings:	Cree cock hackle points tied in 'dun' position.

The second is my own pattern and is basically just a copy of the natural insect.

Hook:	No 8, 10 or 12 long shank.
Silk:	Pearsall's gossamer yellow.
Body:	Fine latex wound over the yellow silk base.
Rib:	Dark peacock herl wound into recesses of segments in the latex and secured with a coinciding rib of fine brass wire.
Hackles:	Two large dark coch-y-bondhu cock hackles wound in together.
Wings:	Cree cock hackle points tied in 'dun' position.
Tails:	Three strands of cock pheasant tail fibre.

Although the use of latex for the body sounds complicated, it is really easy to make. Buy a tube of 'Copydex' glue and spread a series of long, thin strands across a sheet of glass. When they are dry the strands can be peeled off the glass as needed. The latex gives a wonderful translucence to the body, with the base colour of the silk showing through, but turning a yellow-olive colour when seen through the latex. You can substitute furnace hackles for the coch-y-bondhu if you have to, and give the hackles plenty of turns to improve the fly's buoyancy. The peacock herl rib needs to be held down with brass wire if it is not to break and come undone during use. Make sure the wire binds down the herl securely on all turns. The ribs fit neatly into the spiral segments formed between the layers of the latex. It helps, when preparing the latex strips, if you can make them tapered so that the body is given a natural bulge towards the thorax when it is wound in.

I use just one pattern of my own design for the mayfly spinner.

Hook: No 10 or 12 long shank.

Silk: Pearsall's gossamer black.

Body: Pale cream fur (I use the undercoat shed during my elkhound's moult). The last few turns of black base silk should be left exposed at the tail.

Rib: Darkest peacock herl bound down with fine brass wire.

Hackle: Just a few turns of badger cock.

Wings: Badger hackle points tied 'spent'.

Tails: Three strands darkest pheasant tail fibre.

I use my dog's fur because it is exactly the right consistency and colour. Unfortunately elkhounds are rare, so you can substitute any really pale cream pet hair or pale cream wool. Some badger hackles have both a black list and black tips to the fibres. If you can find a cape like this the feathers make ideal mayfly spinner legs.

The grey Wulff is probably the best hatching mayfly nymph pattern.

Hook: No 10 or 12 long shank.

Silk: Brown or grey.

Body: Grey seal's fur.

Wing: A bunch of brown bucktail fibres pulled upwards and forwards as a single wing. (Some later patterns divide the wing).

Tail: Brown bucktail fibres.

I shall give just one mayfly nymph pattern which should be fished submerged.

Hook: No 8, 10, or 12 long shank.

Silk: Pearsall's gossamer olive.

Body: Two or three turns of dyed Canada goose primary wing fibre (see medium olive) tied in at the tail, then the rest of the body and thorax in mid-brown cock pheasant tail fibre (the outer feathers are best).

Rib: Fine brass wire.

Wing cases: Darkest undyed Canada goose primary wing fibre.

Legs: One turn of dark brown hen hackle or soft cock hackle.

Tails: Three strands of cock pheasant tail fibre tied short.

To tie in the body materials, I tie both the goose fibre and the pheasant fibre in at the tail. I then whip the silk a few turns back up the hook towards the eye. Holding the pheasant fibres along the shank, I whip over them with three turns of goose and then whip down with three turns of silk. I then carry on whipping along the body with the silk, binding down the remaining ends of goose, before following over the top with the pheasant fibre. The loose ends can be trimmed near the eye and both fibres are bound down with the wire rib. This gives the nymph a nice fat body.

BLUE WINGED OLIVE

From mid June onwards comes one of the most exciting flies of the dry fly fisherman's season—the blue winged olive. The only fly with which the BWO could be confused is the large spurwing. However, the BWO is much more active on the surface and generally appears in the evening, just before dusk. If a fly is captured the difference is easily spotted, because the BWO has three tails and the spurwing only two.

Because of its activity the BWO is extremely attractive to trout but strangely difficult to imitate. It was G. E. M. Skues who discovered that the orange quill was sometimes remarkably effective 'in certain conditions of light' when trout were rising to the BWO. His pattern recommended condor quill dyed hot orange for the body, and starling feather slips for the wings.

On one particular occasion I had just suffered an evening of utter frustration on the Itchen when the water boiled with rises to the BWO, but I had failed to rise a single fish on the BWO patterns I was using. These included a general imitation of the fly, not unlike a slightly larger medium olive, but with a larger and darker wing, and a Skues-style pattern of the orange quill.

Having read Skues, I was careful to make sure that the fish were rising to duns, rather than nymphs or spinners. There could be no mistake about that! They were rising to duns within inches of my own. It was a salutary lesson which had several compensations. When the light had nearly gone the rise-form changed, and fish started to take spinners. In the gloom I swapped to my own pattern of pheasant tail. I caught a fish at the first cast and another with the second. Although fish were still rising, it was too dark to see or even cast accurately, in the direction of the sound of a rising fish.

When I got home I sat and puzzled. I seemed to have solved the problem of the spinner, but why was my dun refused? I could only put it down to colour. My spinner had been accepted without difficulty. I sat at my fly-tying desk and spread out an array of capes and body materials in front of me. One of the Skues patterns recommended brown seal's fur. The condor quill was supposed to be dyed hot orange and, to be fair, the colour of the quill I used looked more like a dirty brown—but then, after all, the natural BWO body colour is a rather dirty olive-brown.

I thought again of the successful pheasant tail spinner. I had one particularly good pheasant tail feather. It was the deepest rusty-red I have ever seen, and particularly suited to the colour of the sherry spinner. What would a dun look like in this colour? I asked myself. What are the principal features of the natural BWO? First of all, it is an active fly. I am still convinced that the natural's real attraction for the trout is its movement on the surface as it tries to escape the nymphal shuck. Secondly, it is a largish fly—an impression which is enhanced by the size and darkness of its wings when seen on the water. Thirdly, the orange quill seems particularly attractive on an evening when there is that reddish-pink afterglow in the evening sky. Even the bases of the bankside reeds look a deep red in that light. I remembered what Skues had said about 'certain conditions of light'.

My pheasant tail feather would be enhanced by that red of evening—but what about the wings? I searched through my wing feathers. There was nothing exactly the colour of the BWO's wings. Then my eyes lighted on a dyed blue cape of indifferent quality, which was exactly the right colour. I had bought it to hackle iron blues, but it was not much good and did not wind in very well. Why not use hackle-point wings, but tied like a dun instead of spent? This, incidentally, was to be the start of my use of hackle-point wings for all duns.

These would have the additional advantage of movement as the fly traversed the ripples, and would catch any slight breeze there might be to give an impression of movement.

The hackle recommended for the orange quill is a bright ginger-red, and I had just the cape for this—though more red than ginger, more like the colour of conkers, not dissimilar in colour to the pheasant tail for the body. The tails I would make from the spade feathers at the bottom of this cape.

The only decision left was the tying silk. I decided hot orange would be the right colour. The Pearsall's hot orange goes the most marvellous deep translucent orange when varnished with clear cellulose.

I tied three of these flies to begin with, and armed with them I made my way back to Abbotts Barton where I prayed for an evening hatch of BWO. When it happened I caught four fish in less than an hour's fishing. But I was not yet ecstatic. Many writers, including Skues, have warned that one success with an apparently infallible BWO imitation does not mean that the solution has been found.

I fished for several days when the weather was not conducive to BWO hatches. On a day when the weather forecast looked as though it was going to live up to its promise, I took my young son along for a day's fishing. The evening was perfect. There was no wind and there was that rosy glow in the west. Accompanied by our club secretary, Bob Schröder, my son James and I made our way to the main river for the anticipated evening rise.

James was an inexperienced dry fly fisher. I gave him one of my BWO imitations and suggested one of the favourite places for the hatch. As the flies started to drift down, James chose a fish, cast to it and rose it at once. You can imagine my delight. That evening we caught a number of trout.

Since then my pattern of BWO has been infallible. I have given my flies to others who have also had great success with them. I do not understand, any more than Skues did, why this fly should be so deadly—but work it does and it has not failed me yet, even when the evening has been overcast or, as happened recently on several August days, the fly began hatching at about 6 p.m., rather than at sunset.

A summary of the pattern, therefore, is:

Hook:	Mustad 39849 straight-eye size 14.
Silk:	Pearsall's gossamer hot orange.
Body:	Deep rusty-red cock pheasant tail feather fibres.
Rib:	Fine brass wire.

Hackle: Dark ginger-red.
Wings: Dark blue-grey, quite long.
Tails: A few fibres of a spade feather from the hackle cape.

The best pattern for the BWO nymph, particularly in the evening, is one invented by Skues.

Hook: Mustad 39849 size 14.
Silk: Pearsall's gossamer hot orange.
Body: Very dark red-brown wool (Skues recommends cow hair the colour of dried blood).
Rib: Fine brass wire.
Hackle: Very small soft blue-grey hen.
Tails: A few fibres from a dark red cock hackle tied short.

SEDGES

Apart from perhaps the mayfly, sedge patterns give the fisherman a better opportunity of rising larger fish than any other fly, and on occasion will also tempt difficult fish that will look at no other artificial pattern. In a way sedges could often be regarded as a cheat by the dry fly purist, because they will frequently rise fish when there are no natural sedges on the water—even early in the season before any of the common natural sedges have yet appeared.

Most general sedge hatches occur at dusk or after dark, but a sedge pattern can be particularly useful when fishing in sluices or under bridges, or sometimes for rising fish that are burrowing in weed-beds, searching out shrimp or nymphs. Of the estimated 188 British species, there are only five widespread sedges that will commonly be found on the water during the day. Because they are all varying shades of brown or yellow, I only find it necessary to carry three patterns.

My own variation of Skues's little red sedge is:

Hook: Kamasan or Partridge up-eye size 14.
Silk: Pearsall's gossamer hot orange.
Body: Dark fur from a hare's face or ears.
Rib: Fine brass wire.
Body hackle: A long, deep red cock hackle wound right along the body.

Head hackle:	Same colour as body hackle, but slightly larger, tied very bushy.
Wing:	Speckled dark hen pheasant wing section, folded three times and trimmed slightly longer than the hook.

There are many different ways of tying sedges, but I start mine by whipping the silk down the hook to the tail, and then tie in the brass wire and body hackle before dubbing the silk with the hare's fur. I then wind in the body dubbing and leave the silk at the eye end of the hook. This is followed by the body hackle which is left a little short of the eye, bound down with the silk and trimmed off. Both the body hackle and dubbing are secured with open turns of brass wire, secured behind the eye with silk. Having cut a suitable length of hen pheasant wing material, I roll it up to make a scroll with three turns. I pinch the thinnest (outer) end between index finger and thumb and hold it along the hook shank with my fingers just behind the hook eye.

A loop of silk is formed and pulled down between finger and thumb three times, so that the wing root is bound firmly down on the shank. I then closely whip the silk back up to the hook eye, giving a neat binding over the top of the wing roots and making a stable base for the head hackle, which is wound from the eye to the rearmost turn of silk securing the wings. Before tying in the wings you may prefer to divide the top half of the body hackle, leaving a 'V'-shaped groove to accept the wing. Finally the wing is trimmed off at an oblique angle to leave it projecting a little beyond the bend of the hook.

I find my version of a dark sedge very useful when a bigger fly is needed, particularly for bringing up large, dour trout which are used to a diet of fry and are usually found buried in submerged tree roots or in the depths of turbulent sluices.

Hook:	Partridge or Kamasan up-eye size 12.
Silk:	Pearsall's gossamer black.
Body:	Pale pet fur mixed with a hint of pink wool.
Rib:	Fine brass wire.
Body hackle:	Dark furnace cock.
Head hackle:	As for body but a little larger.
Wing:	Darkest section of Canada goose primary wing, doubled.

The third useful pattern is my version of the cinnamon sedge.

Hook:	Partridge or Kamasan up-eye size 12 or 14.
Silk:	Pearsall's gossamer mid-brown.
Body:	Three strands of the lighter section of Canada goose primary wing.
Rib:	Fine brass wire.
Body hackle:	Ginger cock.
Head hackle:	As for body but slightly larger.
Wing:	Scrolled feather from underside of cock pheasant wing, well mottled.

If you fish a river that is particularly prolific in sedges, you may find you need more patterns or size variations than the three I have listed, but I find that these suit every circumstance I have met so far.

BLACK GNAT

There are a few land-bred flies which are habitués of water or which live close by and are frequently blown into it, therefore being of interest to fishermen. Of these, four principal ones stand out: the black gnat; the hawthorn fly; the daddy-long-legs and the alder. Of these there is no doubt that the most significant on the chalk stream is the black gnat. Although there is a large number of patterns to imitate the black gnat, the natural is surprisingly hard to copy. Incidentally, the fly is neither a gnat nor is it black, although it is such a dark brown colour that black is usually used in the dressings to imitate it. I find the fly is best fished floating just within the surface film, so I leave the hackle very sparse.

Hook:	Kamasan up-eye size 18.
Silk:	Pearsall's gossamer black.
Body:	Black tying silk with two turns of black ostrich herl at the shoulder.
Hackle:	Two turns of small black cock.
Rib:	Fine silver wire.
Wings:	Small dark starling wing feather with pale tip.

The natural fly has wings like a house fly, a flat 'V' extending outwards across the back. If you look at the small outside feathers of a starling's wing you will find just a few with a light tip and with an equal quantity of flue each side of the quill. Prepare the feather by removing most of the flue and leaving just enough of the quill protruding for tying in. Place the feather on top of the hook, with the quill pointing forward over the eye. Bind the feather down with a few turns of silk, then pull the quill forwards so that the feather fibres are narrowed where they are squeezed by the binding. Cut a small 'V' in the back of the feather fibre so that it gives the impression of being two wings.

HAWTHORN FLY

Although only in season for a short time, the hawthorn fly is frequently blown on the water late in April and early in May. Its struggles to get free are very attractive to trout, so it is well worth carrying a pattern early in the season. The hawthorn looks like an overgrown black gnat, with large, dangly hind legs. Many patterns imitate these legs, but I have not found this necessary. The male and female differ in wing colour, but I usually see more males, which have pale wings, so my pattern imitates these. I tie the fly sedge-style, with a hackled body and scrolled wing, but the wings are trimmed to an arrowhead shape when viewed from above, pointing towards the back of the hook, but slightly shorter than the hook.

Hook:	Partridge or Kamasan up-eye size 14.
Silk:	Pearsall's gossamer black.
Body:	Black ostrich herl.
Rib:	Fine silver wire.
Body hackle:	Black cock.
Head hackle:	As body but slightly larger.
Wing:	Pale grey pigeon wing feather fibre, scrolled three times.

DADDY-LONG-LEGS

Although various species of crane fly will be found on the water during much of the fishing season, I find this pattern works best in the autumn, and it will sometimes tempt large opportunist fish which are not usually fly takers.

Hook:	Long shank size 10 or 12.
Silk:	Pearsall's gossamer pale brown.

Body:	Natural raffia.
Rib:	Fine brass wire.
Legs:	Six long cock pheasant tail fibres, each knotted in the middle.
Hackle:	Two turns large ginger cock.
Wings:	Two large mid-brown cock hackles tied 'spent'.

To tie the fly, whip the silk down the hook in the usual way, then tie in the raffia and brass wire. Whip the raffia back towards the hook eye but leave it short to allow room for the wings and hackle. Wind in the wire to segment the body, following the pattern of turns in the raffia. Trim off raffia and wire after securing with whipping silk. Holding a pair of the prepared legs (thin end pointing towards the hook bend) on each side of the hook shank, tie them in with three turns of silk. Then tie in the wings as for a spent spinner. Now tie in the four other legs (paired on each side of the hook but pointing towards the hook eye) with three or four turns of silk, then tie in the hackle over the leg whippings. Finish off with several turns of silk to form a head tapering towards the hook eye, but avoid trapping the legs in the silk as you whip.

ALDER

Although the alder seems to be a popular fly among still water fishermen in particular, and is fished wet on many acid streams, I have never seen the fly taken on a chalk stream although they are regularly to be found struggling on the water. I have seen several floating over fish, but they have always been ignored. As a result I have never bothered to tie one.

Although I described the alder as a land-bred fly, it might better be described as an amphibian because the eggs are laid on bankside trees and when the larva hatches it crawls into the water where it lives until ready to hatch a year later. The larva crawls up the bank and buries itself deep in the mud to pupate, emerging after a few weeks as an adult fly. As I personally have found the alder useless as a fisherman's fly I shall not attempt to suggest a pattern, simply because I cannot recommend one that works!

Many trout fishermen will probably disagree with my selection. 'Why didn't he include Greenwell's Glory?' they will ask. 'Why isn't there a pattern for the small dark olive?' As I said at the beginning of this chapter, I have included only the flies I use myself. There are thousands of fly patterns, and many regional variations of these.

The flies I have listed are more than I use in any one season on the chalk streams, but they are all patterns I have either invented, modified or copied, and I have used all of them and know that they will all catch fish for me.

While there are many 'fancy' patterns (which are designed as a general suggestion of several flies), I have found that all but the pheasant tail spinner seem to be lacking in some respect. This does not mean that I consider them ineffective, it just means that they do not work for me.

I have tried to give patterns that contain only easily available materials and which require the minimum of dyeing. I worry a great deal about fly patterns which recommend dyeing, because it is very hard to predict what colour will be achieved. My recommendation of the use of flavine dye has the advantage of actually painting colour onto a feather, so it is possible to see the colour you are achieving while you are adding the dye.

The two books on flies I have recommended, the *Dictionary of Trout Flies* and *Trout Fly Recognition*, will more than make up for any omissions in my list.

Chapter Seven

Generally speaking, the better the chalk stream you fish, the greater the problem you will have with drag. Chalk streams with good rates of flow and prolific growths of weed inevitably produce varying rates of current, which causes drag.

Fish that are feeding on free-floating duns and nymphs have stationed themselves in the ideal position to intercept food as it is delivered to them by the current. They know where their food will appear and how it will be carried to them. They are familiar with the eccentricities of the current as it washes towards the lie. They even seem to be able to discern the difference between the erratic movement of a natural fly blown by a gusty wind, and the unpredictable behaviour of an artificial that is being dragged by the weight of current against the fisherman's line or leader.

When the dry fly man has his artificial refused, he usually blames it initially on one of two things: he is either fishing the wrong fly, or he has cast clumsily or inaccurately. But drag is probably more responsible than any other factor. Because the fisherman cannot see that his fly is dragging, he is inclined to believe that it is not. As a result he will change his fly, or try casting again with greater delicacy and accuracy. He may on occasion blame himself for being seen by the fish.

If a fish is rising regularly to naturals and the fisherman is using a reasonable facsimile, it is worth studying the pattern of the flow over the lie and the path that the naturals follow when riding on the current. If he can put his fly next to a natural and see how the two behave, so much the better. Nine times out of ten he will see his own fly follow a different path from the natural.

Just because his fly does not leave a wake on the surface of the stream or, on occasion, does not even seem to divert from the natural line, is no indication that it is not dragging. A loop in the leader close to the fly, or even a twist in the point, will be sufficient to make the fly behave unnaturally when the trace lands on the surface. The smallest twitch or movement in the wrong direction can be sufficient to warn a feeding fish. Very often the fish will not be put down by such a movement, but it will be enough to tell him that he is not looking at the natural insect and therefore that it is not worth eating.

I recently moved from my old fishing haunt of more than ten years on the Itchen. My new water is much higher up, where the river is wider, shallower, and faster, with considerably more weed. There is more insect life here, with more native fish and many more runs and eddies providing ideal feeding positions.

When I first fished this water I was aware of the problem of drag when it was obvious, but to begin with I could not understand why the patterns I had used on my old water no longer seemed to be effective. I was not casting any differently and the trout in my old stamping-ground seemed to find my patterns irresistible under the right circumstances.

It was not until there was a really good hatch of medium olives that I could see the problem. As my artificial floated down among the naturals it would make a small move to one side or the other. Sometimes this was caused by the current pulling on the leader where it had partially landed upstream of the fly; sometimes it was because the leader fell on a slightly streamier run, and sometimes because the current close to me was moving faster than the water where the fish was feeding, making a belly in the fly line and pulling the artificial off course. These movements were often hardly perceptible, although they were obviously a blatant diversion from the trout's angle.

On some occasions, I discovered, a small move up or downstream would remedy the problem. On other occasions it was necessary to let the fly land just upstream of the fish, so that it would not drag until it had passed over the lie. More than anything else, I learned that extremely accurate and well-timed casting was called for.

Under the far bank on one of the bends, fish line up to sip down spinners in the evening. Between my bank and these fish there are three main differences in the rate of flow. Below my feet the water is slow-moving and is diverted in several directions by large banks of starwort. Farther out, huge beds of ranunculus divide the water into small, fast runs with glassy, slower moving glides upstream of each plant. On the other side the main flow of the river sweeps round the outside of the bend, carrying the majority of the flies to the waiting fish.

In such a situation the major problem in casting to these fish is their distance from you. It is a long cast with an eight-and-a-half foot rod and a No 5 or 6 line. However, if you time it right and the breeze is not too contrary, it is usually possible to land a fly with reasonable precision above a rising fish. The problem is evident almost immediately, for as soon as the fly lands, the current starts to pull first on the leader and then on the rest of the line. The problem with drag on the leader can be alleviated by arresting the line just before the fly lands on the water, allowing the leader to rebound towards the caster and land with a snaky pattern on the surface. Some of this snaky pattern can sometimes also be imparted to the far end of the fly line.

Usually this is not sufficient to stop the drag. However, a cast that is made forming a belly upstream and imparting the snaky pattern to the end of the line and leader will sometimes do the trick, but it is by no means easy to do this while at the same time attempting to gain the maximum distance. Sometimes just moving a few yards up or downstream will help but, because of the distance involved, one normally wants to be as nearly opposite the fish's lie as possible.

As you should know, when casting a dry fly the usual method of getting the fly to make a soft landing is to aim at a point about a foot in the air above the place where you want the fly to land. If you do this, the line and leader straighten nicely and the fly, leader and line then drop gently on the surface. One method of getting slack in the leader, which may give the fly a chance to swim naturally before drag sets in, is to aim at a point about three feet above the surface. This results in the fly falling backwards towards the angler, leaving a series of curves in the leader and the fly line. This option can be useful when casting at full stretch to a distant target.

Small whirlpools also present a problem. When a natural fly is caught in these it spins round in the natural flow, but when the drag of a leader and line is added, your own fly often pulls out of the whirl in exactly the wrong direction. This is a particular problem when fishing close to the bank. Any small projection or weed raft produces whirlpools, and they are frequently over a good lie. This is where timing comes in. If one studies the flow past an obstruction it will be noted that the whirlpools occur at fairly regular intervals. The trick is to place the fly between them and trust to luck that the leader is not caught in another that may be spinning slightly farther out.

It is impossible to overcome all the problems of drag, but many can be mastered by a careful study of the surface pattern. The important thing is to decide where to cast from, even if that casting position is not so ideal in terms of distance, camouflage or allowing room for the back-cast.

After moving to my new beat on the Itchen it took me some weeks to settle in, but eventually I noticed that the fish seemed to be less sensitive to drag when I was fishing a nymph.

I normally like to fish my nymphs inert, particularly the Skues patterns, which are designed as an imitation of the insect just before hatching and are therefore naturally immobile. Thus the technique for fishing them is virtually identical to fishing the dry fly. One would expect, therefore, that drag would be as off-putting as with the dry fly.

This does not appear to be the case, however. I have said that the problem of drag can be surmounted in several ways, but on my present water there are occasions when it is impossible to overcome it completely. In these cases I have found it hopeless attempting to catch fish that are lying in these seemingly impossible positions.

After some weeks of experimenting, however, I found that those fish that could not be caught with a dry fly would often come to a nymph, even though they were feeding on duns. Why they should be less sensitive to drag when it was apparent in a nymph, which should naturally be inert, remains a mystery to me.

I described earlier one section of my water where I had to cast at full stretch to reach fish rising under the opposite bank. I found the drag problem on this section of the river impossible to overcome because of the multiplicity of currents between myself and the fish, and because of the casting distance involved. In my early days on the new fishery I was standing in this place and was watching a good fish rising regularly to duns that were drifting along close to the bank.

I tried several times to cover the fish with a dry pale watery, but drag set in as soon as the fly landed, and was so bad that the fish was put down for a while. I waited until it started rising again and tied on a nymph. After a few unsuccessful attempts I managed to cover the fish. Although the nymph, too, was being dragged away from its lie, the trout turned and snapped at it. I landed a fish of one-and-a-half pounds.

Elsewhere on the water, where the drag problem was not so acute, I tried fishing a nymph to a trout rising to pale watery duns, but without success. When I tried with a floating imitation of the pale watery there was no hesitation and the fish rose to the artificial at once. I even tried dragging the nymph under these circumstances, but it still produced no result.

The only explanation I can think of is that the current under the far bank made free-floating natural nymphs behave in a similar manner to my dragging artificial. But this was not a one-off. In several other places, with similar drag problems, the nymph was taken.

Extraordinarily, I found the same later on, when fish were taking the BWO in the evening. I have found that BWO hatches promote more selectivity in trout than any other fly. If fish are taking the nymph they will not usually be tempted by the dun, and they are not interested in the nymph when feeding on duns or spinners.

Yet on this evening there were several trout under the opposite bank taking every dun that came over them. The drag problem was the same with the artificial dun, so, armed with the knowledge gleaned earlier in the day, I put on a nymph and rose the first fish that I covered properly, despite the drag.

At such distances it is very difficult to hook fish, and it is sometimes difficult to detect the nymph being taken, particularly in fading light. Despite this I managed to rise three fish and hook one of them, all on the BWO nymph, and on every occasion the nymph was dragging, although not in the same direction every time.

When I cannot find an explanation for a problem like this I always feel a bit of a cheat taking fish in such a manner, but I shall persevere and perhaps a solution will present itself. The whole dilemma seems to revolve around the activity, or lack of it, in the natural nymph. Perhaps the natural is not always inactive when approaching the surface to hatch, although most observers seem to believe that the fly is inert until it starts to struggle out of the nymphal shuck.

This brings me to the subject of impossible fish in general. Some writers on fishing like to describe the fish they have caught and the remarkable brain power they have brought to bear to solve an apparently insoluble problem, so I thought it would be refreshing to describe just two of the many fish that I have not been able to catch. They stand out more vividly in my memory than many of those that have succumbed.

At the Abbotts Barton Club water the top end of one of the carriers was my favourite beat. To me it had everything. It was wild, but without offering insurmountable jungles of vegetation, and because only the right bank (when viewed upstream) was fishable, it suited me as a left-hander. There was a spinney that grew down to the water on the opposite bank, and the whole beat was full of pools and ripples that ran under the overhanging branches of the trees opposite.

The beat was approached over the sill of a sluice, where another carrier branched off across the meadows. Just beyond the sluice was a large tree and then a stretch of a few yards of bank before the interruption of another, much smaller tree. On the upstream side of this tree, under my own bank, there was a trout of good size. It lay in relatively shallow water that was partly guarded by the foliage of the little tree and partly by the bankside growth.

The problem the fish posed was a double one. It was extremely shy and would therefore not tolerate the fisherman coming too close, but the larger tree near the sluice severely restricted the back-cast, so only a short line could be used to cast to the fish. I first saw the fish quite early in the season, before most of the bankside cover had grown up. Unfortunately it saw me at the same time, so that as I ducked it sped into its secret lair.

I carried on upstream to fish but made a mental note of the fish's position, promising myself that I would return later. This top beat has only one path, so those returning from fishing higher up are forced to walk close to the edge of the bank, thus putting down any fish that may be feeding downstream.

On my return along the path I looked downstream and could see that the fish was once again in position near the little tree. I watched for a while from some distance. It was lying very close to the bank, with the main current flowing a little farther out. The fish was looking for flies in this current and was swinging out to take both duns and nymphs as they swept by. The trout was obviously not a fussy one— anything edible was fair game.

Because it was lying so close to the bank I thought I could probably crawl past and then get into a position where I might be able to cover the fish. I crept past the lie until I was almost in the shadow of the large tree, but to no avail—the fish had gone. I decided to fish elsewhere and come back in the evening.

When I returned, I dropped to my hands and knees while I was still under the large tree. I moved nearer the water so that I could slide one leg over the bank and peer past the immature growth from the small tree and the few nettles that were sprouting from the bank. The fish was there and was occasionally rising to something invisible in the surface. The growing gloom of evening was accentuated by the shadows of the trees in the spinney on the opposite bank. It is surprising how fading light strikes the angler with a sense of urgency. Because the duns of evening were not yet visible on the surface, I decided to tie on a small dark hare's fur nymph and give the fish a try.

I moved up a little and began false casting to work out enough line to cover the fish. Just a few switches of the rod were all that were needed to send the trout into its bolt-hole among the adjacent weeds.

In just one day I realised that I had a campaign on my hands. I simply cannot resist a difficult fish. It is the challenge. No matter how much time I wasted, I had to catch that fish! I cannot explain it, but for a week I dreamt of that trout. How could I overcome the problem of the back-cast? Even a side-cast would not allow the line to pass the overhanging branches of the large tree where they swept out over the water behind me. As I saw it, the only solution was to get closer to the fish, which meant a shorter back-cast and the benefits of a shorter forward one, too.

I shall not bore you with the number of occasions when I approached this fish, only to scare it as soon as I lifted my rod. Just once or twice I managed to place a fly about right, but as soon as the line touched the water the trout took off. It was becoming an obsession. I had already decided that this was to be my last year at Abbotts Barton—if I were to have the fish, it would have to be this season.

One day, when the sun was just right to mask my approach to this most difficult fish, I succeeded in persuading it to take a medium olive. It had failed to detect my presence and my subsequent false casts. The fly landed just right, about a foot above the trout's position, and swam jauntily down on the current as it flowed past the lie. It was with intense excitement that I saw the fish drift out from under the bank, lift its nose, then open its mouth and swallow the fly. I lifted the rod to set the hook, but there was nothing there—no contact. The fish bolted into its hidy-hole. Although I returned several times, and usually found the fish in its feeding position, I never again succeeded in covering it with a successful cast.

At the end of the season I resigned to take up a rod on a different water farther upstream. Although I have returned to Abbotts Barton as a guest several times since then, I have not seen the fish. The movement of silt and different weed growths have changed the pattern of the water and that particular spot no longer offers a good lie for a fish.

Since moving to my new water I have been engaged in a similar campaign, but with different problems. The average size of fish in the water I now fish is smaller than those at Abbotts Barton, but there is one fish I have located that is big for the water and lies out in the middle of the river, sheltered in a natural hollow within a bed of starwort.

Despite its size this fish is free rising, and the abundant fly hatches on this stretch of the river mean that my quarry sometimes rises for much of the day. There are three problems offered by this fish's position. The first is a question of cover, for although there is a jungle of vegetation behind the bank to trap a dipping back-cast, there is little growth on the edge of the river at this spot to camouflage the fisherman. The fish is sensitive to movement on the bank, so a longish cast is necessary from the cover of the nearest suitable bush. The second problem is one of drag. The trout's lie within the bed of starwort is ideal, because the current forms a bow wave in front of the weed, slowing down the flow and giving the fish ample opportunity to study any fly that crosses the feeding area. The water between the bank and the starwort bed is fast-flowing, so tends to drag the fly away before it has properly covered the fish. Finally, part of the bed of starwort, between the angler and fish's lie, is close to the surface and tends to trap debris that has been carried down by the current. This snags the line, sinks the fly and aggravates the drag.

For several weeks I cast to this fish, but the problem of drag and a gusty breeze meant that I could never cover the trout properly. If the fly dragged across its lie the fish would stop feeding, although I could still see it sitting close to the bottom of its secure lie. On other occasions I managed to land the fly satisfactorily, but the fish was not convinced by it, so that although it continued to rise to naturals it would not take my artificial. Several changes of fly were called for, because the one I was using would become caught on some of the trapped debris on the starwort and therefore begin to sink on subsequent casts.

On a day near the end of last season, I decided to spend as long as was necessary to capture this fish. I made myself comfortable out of sight on the bank, waiting for the fly hatch to begin. After a while a few medium olive duns and some pale wateries began to appear. Typically, another fish began to rise, between me and the fish in the starwort. If I ignored this fish and cast to the farther one, once it had started to rise, my line would be bound to spook the nearer fish which was then likely to bolt and put down the other one.

I decided to fish to the nearest one first and eventually caught it, but, needless to say, once hooked, the fish shot straight across to the patch of starwort and I saw my primary target bolt upstream and disappear into a patch of ribbon weed some yards higher up. After a good fight I netted out the first fish, which surprised me because it weighed over two pounds.

Determined not to be put off, I sat down and waited. If I gave it long enough I was sure the principal trout would return and would eventually start to rise again. The fly hatch dwindled and gradually petered out, but there was still no sign of my trout. Reflections on the surface prevented me from seeing if the fish was back in its lie among the starwort; I would just have to be patient and hope for another hatch.

I crawled away from my vantage point and walked to my car to get my sandwiches. I might just as well have lunch while I was waiting. By the time I returned I was delighted to see that the fish was rising—but what to? There were no duns on the surface, and closer inspection of the rise-form showed the fish sipping at something just in the film. There were no spinners around so I studied the water as it flowed past my vantage point, hoping to spot a nymph or two that might give me a hint. I could see nothing. The fish continued to rise so I decided to tie on my dark hare's fur nymph, which is usually my first choice in these circumstances.

My first cast left plenty of slack in the leader and the nymph dropped in a position upstream of the fish's last rise. It drifted down, right across the lie, but there was no visible reaction. At my third attempt I thought I saw a slight movement under water so I tightened, but there was nothing there. The fish stopped rising. I waited again and munched on a sandwich. Two fish began to rise higher up and, as there was no sign of activity from my protagonist, I crept away from the bank and made my way up to try the other fish.

I returned early in the evening. There were a few early blue winged olives and some medium olives floating down, but nothing was rising to them. Then I saw my target make a customary rise in the film. I put on a BWO nymph and covered the fish several times, but there was no response, although the trout continued to rise sporadically to something invisible.

In desperation I decided to change to a little red sedge. It is a fly with a reputation for bringing up sulky fish. I cast two or three times, but each time the position either wasn't quite right or drag set in before the fly floated over the fish. Drag is not always a bad thing with a sedge—on occasion it can make the fly look lifelike—but there was still no response. I lengthened the line by a couple more feet to allow for a little extra slack in the leader to take up the drag. The fish had stopped rising and I did not hold out much hope. The fly landed and cocked nicely. It floated down and there was an eruption. I was taken so completely by surprise that I struck much too hard; there was a moment's resistance, then the line flew backwards and landed in a coil on the water in front of me.

The fly had gone and so had my fish—but he'll be back next season and so shall I.

My present fishing is just how I like it. The banks are not trimmed and the water-weed is cut only enough to prevent excessive growth above the surface. I am sure that this helps to retain the natural fly life, and once the banks have grown up there is ample cover for the fisherman.

Some pussy willow saplings got a little out of hand last year, so I cut those down. They were not along the edge of the water, but formed a straggly line a few yards back. They had made casting quite impossible for about 50 yards, and since there were three or four fish which rose regularly in that stretch, my pruning activities were designed to make them more accessible. Like everywhere else on the water, the current here is complex and it is difficult to avoid drag, even when fishing directly upstream. Although it was possible to get quite close to these fish while they were rising, casting to them had been out of the question because of the restricted room behind.

I had undertaken my pruning activities while waiting for the evening rise. There was a spinner fall at about 7 p.m. and the fish started rising along the 50 yards. Although I had left the bankside cover largely untouched, each rising fish was put down as soon as I was in a position to cast. Despite many subsequent precautions to conceal my approach, I failed to rise any of the fish in this section of the water.

The only conclusion I can draw is that my own silhouette had been masked by the saplings before they were pruned and that, no matter how cautious my approach, the fish could see me clearly once the willows were down. This is all the more confusing because behind the willows there are other much larger trees which, from the fishes' viewpoint, completely mask the lighted horizon. I noticed, towards the end of the season, that there were no fish lying in the 50 yards but

I do not know whether the abundant weed growth later in the year made their lies unsuitable, or whether the more open aspect led them to find somewhere more secure.

This incident has made me question the whole business of bank cutting, tree trimming and general fishery maintenance. At my previous fishery, which in later years was democratically run, the average age of the members gradually went up. New members, who were prepared to pay for the fishing and were able to take advantage of a potential four fishing weekdays or three 'weekend' days per week, were usually retired. I am not suggesting that the retired are necessarily infirm, but well-cut banks and easy casting definitely become more of a priority with advancing years.

The result of the club's democracy meant that the majority wanted the banks cleared, lower branches of the trees lopped and the wilder parts of the fishery generally tidied up. Who can blame the members? When I reach their age I shall no longer want to struggle through a jungle in order to cast to a fish protected by overhanging branches. The problem is that fish which are now stocked in that water do not hang around for long; after each stocking the general drift of the population is downstream. Because of the increase in silting, which has removed many of the natural lies in the water, and the policy of stripping away any obstruction that may impede easy fishing access to the water, the trout population no longer feels secure—indeed, there are few places where fish can lie without feeling threatened. The end result is that the trout vote with their fins and drift downstream in search of somewhere more hospitable.

Even more surprising is a policy that has recently been introduced on the same water. An annual meeting of members agreed to a proposal that any fish caught, which were over the 14-inch size limit, must be killed. It is all the more astonishing that this decision should have been taken on a fishery which prides itself on the fact that the water was once fished by G. E. M. Skues. Skues resigned from that fishery nearly eighty years ago because he disagreed with a policy to introduce stock fish.

The argument for the killing of all takeably-sized fish was advanced on the grounds that fish caught and returned were unlikely to survive. It seems extraordinary to me that such an argument can be justified when so-called 'catch and release' waters, both in this country and the United States, have shown huge increases in the numbers of native fish, many of which must have been caught and returned to the water several times.

The only explanation I can think of for this rule is that it is an attempt to relieve fishing pressure on the water by sending some members home early when they have caught their limit.

What bothers me is that the genuine wild Itchen trout is probably close to extinction. The river has been stocked for years with over-weight farm-bred fish, most of which probably come from hatcheries on the river Test or elsewhere.

Native Itchen fish are beautifully delicate creatures. They have no hint of yellow on their undersides; they have long, tapering pectoral fins and huge tails; they are long for their weight and have a delightful display of red spots along the lateral line, and the anal fins have a bright white line along their leading edges. Fish of 14 inches probably weigh little more than a pound, but if left to grow and thrive would most likely attain a weight of about two pounds. No matter what club you belong to or what rules it imposes, I trust you will never kill such a fish if you catch one. I beg you, admire it and then return it to the river of its birth, where it may breed others just like it. After all, if it is returned to the water there is a chance it will survive. If it is banged on the head there is no question that the Itchen will lose another native.

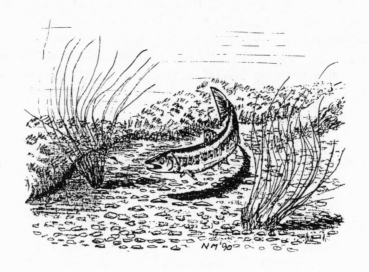

Chapter Eight

The one aspect of fly fishing that I have so far only touched upon is fishing the nymph. For many years the rules of chalk stream fishing did not allow the fishing of a wet fly in any form.

Probably since fly fishing began, flies had been fished by casting them across the river and then allowing the speed of current to tow the line, and therefore the fly, across and downstream—the method still used on most British and Irish rain-fed rivers. A different method that was found to be effective gradually grew up on the chalk streams and culminated in the exclusive use of the dry fly. The rivers Test and Itchen became the temples to the art of upstream dry fly fishing, and the famous fisherman and entomologist, F. M. Halford, was the high priest.

Fly fishing's renaissance on the southern chalk streams occurred in the late nineteenth and early twentieth centuries, and one of its leading lights was Mr Halford. His contribution to the understanding of water flies and their life-cycle cannot be understated, but he had one weakness—he was blind to the opportunities offered by the wet fly and closed his mind to any suggestion that there was a genuine case for its use.

Even during Halford's time it was known that much of the food eaten by trout was captured under water. Despite this it was regarded as unsporting to fish wet flies on the chalk streams. It is reasonable to regard the downstream wet fly as unsporting, because there is no question that it results in a large number of 'pricked' fish (touched by the hook point) and also involves significant disturbance to the water. On rain-fed trout rivers, the natural turbulence and lack of fishing pressure makes the fishing of downstream wet flies both acceptable and practical.

Everyone on the chalk streams seemed to accept Halford's unquestioning exclusivity of the dry fly, and most fishing clubs on the Test and Itchen imposed the upstream dry fly rule on their members.

However, a London solicitor, G. E. M. Skues, who had the good fortune to fish the River Itchen at Abbotts Barton and was a devotee of Halford, noticed frequent occasions when fish were apparently rising, but took no interest in the dry fly. On one occasion Skues caught a fish on an accidentally sunken dry fly and his subsequent experiments, observations and studies convinced him that there could be no ethical objection to fishing imitations of nymphs provided they were fished upstream in a similar manner to the dry fly, and were fished to trout that were obviously feeding on nymphs.

To a certain extent Halford had been a hypocrite over the nymph controversy. The gold ribbed hare's ear is undoubtedly a copy of the hatching medium olive and therefore, strictly speaking, is a nymph pattern. Halford recommended this fly, but in order to satisfy his dry fly bigotry his pattern was tied with wings!

It is now a fact of history that Skues' arguments in favour of nymph fishing gradually gained general acceptance, with the result that today nymph fishing is permitted on virtually all the chalk streams and has come a long way, thanks largely to a former river Avon keeper, Frank Sawyer. Skues' nymphs were designed to imitate insect larvae just before hatching and were therefore fished close to the surface and inert. Frank Sawyer saw opportunities for fishing nymphs in an earlier stage of development. Most ephemerid nymphs are very agile little creatures which dart about among the weeds capturing the river detritus as it is washed along by the current.

Sawyer developed his own pattern of nymphs which were fished upstream but were designed to sink to the depths where these agile nymphs were most commonly found and where, therefore, trout were most likely to be found feeding on them. Having established that fine copper wire was the best way of weighting these nymphs and building up the body shape, he then had to arrive at a method of giving the nymphs the vital appearance of agility that would trigger the predatory instincts of the trout.

He did this by developing the 'induced take' method of fishing nymphs. The idea was to cast sufficiently upstream of a fish to allow time for the nymph to sink to the chosen trout's depth. Just as the nymph was approaching the fish, he gave the rod a slight upward twitch. The nymph gave a corresponding underwater twitch which induced the trout to snap at it.

Now in theory this all sounds very simple, but in practice it is far from easy. The first thing to master in fishing a sunken nymph is to persuade the fly to sink at all, and then to sink it to the required depth. The matter of sinking is assisted by weighting the nymph, but it is important that the leader should offer as little resistance to the water as possible. Fortunately, natural nymphs are streamlined so that their movement through the water requires the minimum effort, and artificial nymphs should be similarly designed. Sawyer chose to tie his nymphs without hackles as imitations of legs, unlike the Skues nymphs. He also advocated the use of fish slime (if you had already caught one) to wipe over the leader and nymphs to aid sinking. In the absence of fish slime he recommended wiping the leader with saliva or mud.

It is typical of Frank Sawyer's down-to-earth approach to fishing that he preferred to say he was 'pitching' a nymph rather than 'casting' it. But this expression describes exactly the casting action needed to get a nymph to sink quickly. He recommended a technique that is similar to casting the dry fly, but as the line shoots through the rod rings it should be arrested so that the fly hits the water before the line and leader, penetrating the surface film and dragging the leader down with it. This action must be tempered with delicacy, however, so that the nymph penetrates the surface without causing a splash.

There are two basic problems posed by fishing a deep nymph. The first is gauging the speed of the current. A nymph will only sink at a specific rate, according to its weight, shape and the resistance of the leader. It is therefore necessary to judge how far ahead of the fish it must be pitched in order to be carried down to the trout's position. Because the fisherman is unlikely to be able to see his nymph once it has sunk, he has considerable difficulty judging where it is in the water, and its position in relation to the trout.

The second problem is deciding when the nymph is sufficiently close to the fish in order to give the twitch that will trigger the trout's predatory instinct. There is a further problem—that of seeing the fish and recognising when it has taken the fly.

On a bright, sunlit day the fisherman may be able to witness the whole process and time it all correctly, but bright, sunlit days are a relative rarity so that usually a lot of guesswork is involved. Detecting when the nymph has been taken is even more difficult. In my experience there is a sort of sixth sense that seems to take over. The initial twitch is given when you think the nymph is approaching the fish, and setting the hook becomes almost instinctive.

Having said how difficult it is, I have found with experience that quite suddenly you seem to 'know' when the nymph has been taken. Don't ask me to explain because I cannot. Sometimes you will actually see that the remainder of the leader, which is still floating, has been arrested momentarily; sometimes there will be a muted flash from the fish's mouth as it opens and closes on the nymph, or there will be some indication as the fish turns to take the nymph. But on other occasions you just 'know'. I have discussed this phenomenon with many good nymph fishermen and none seems to know what signal he received—he just knew he should tighten on the line to set the hook.

Fishing Skues pattern nymphs is somewhat simpler, because the nymph is closer to the surface and very often the surface will be disturbed as the fish takes the fly. But this cannot be counted on and Skues himself knew the nymph fisherman's sixth sense, although he described the turn of a trout to intercept a nymph as 'a little brown wink under water'. Even so, you will surprise yourself when, for the first time, you tighten the line instinctively and find you have hooked a nymphing fish.

Towards the end of the last season the fish were particularly difficult on the Itchen. The water was low and clear and hatches of duns were relatively sparse, but there were several rise-forms as fish disturbed the surface. Occasional dorsal fins and tails broke the surface in a leisurely fashion as the fish went about their feeding ritual. I covered several trout with dry flies but they took no interest and, as is my wont in these circumstances, I attached one of my small, dark hare's fur nymphs.

One particular fish caught my attention. It was rising regularly on the other side of the river, its nose just disturbing the underside of the surface film, but never actually breaking it. I had seen a fish in this position many times before but had decided it was a small escapee rainbow from an upstream trout farm. On a couple of previous occasions I had seen the glint of a rosy cheek which is a sure indication of a rainbow (there is an agreement on the Itchen that no rainbows should be stocked).

Sometimes the fish would show its dorsal fin, at others its tail. I had greased the leader down to the point, so that the nymph would swim just below the surface but, because it took several casts to cover the fish accurately, the first two or three inches of the leader had started to sink. As there had been no result from my previous casts I lengthened the line by no more than a foot, and dropped the nymph just upstream of the position of the last rise.

I was concentrating carefully on the nymph's position as it swam down in the fast current under the far bank. As the nymph passed my estimation of the fish's position, I tightened. I 'knew' the fish had taken it. There was no indication from the leader nor was there any movement on the surface, nor had I seen Skues' 'little brown wink under water'—there was just a feeling of utter certainty that the nymph had been taken. After a magnificent fight I landed a rainbow of two pounds two ounces—much larger than any rainbow trout I had previously caught on this water. I suspect it had been in that position for at least two years after escaping as a small table-sized farm fish.

Earlier on the same day the light had been perfect to watch several fish nymphing. There is no question that if you offer them a good approximation of what they want they are less fussy over presentation and drag, and seem to be less wary generally.

One of these fish was a good distance away, lying just out from some brick piling on the opposite bank. It was taking everything that came past it and was typical of an autumn fish, anxious to gain every morsel to put on weight before the predations of winter and the annual spawning cycle. It was a long cast but I covered it after several attempts. I could see the fish quite clearly as it snapped at my nymph, but because of the distance involved I did not hook it securely. I tightened, and the fish flapped on the surface for a moment before turning over and coming off.

I moved a few yards upstream with the intention of casting to a familiar friend that I had been after all season. I watched this fish for a while in the hope of overcoming what seemed to be insuperable problems of drag, complicated by weed sprouts growing through the surface. Within just a few minutes the fish I had hooked and lost began to rise again. I ducked behind the bushes on the bank to recover my former casting position and dropped my nymph upstream of the trout. The fish took it and this time I made firm contact.

Quite why a fish that had so recently been through the trauma of being hooked and lost on a nymph should recover its composure so quickly I do not understand. Those that are hooked and lost on a dry fly are far more chary about rising again than those that have been fooled and lost on a nymph. I have often noticed that fish which have been frightened by a dry fly will often begin nymphing but will ignore floating flies for some time after they have resumed feeding.

Casting a Skues nymph is really more like fishing a dry fly, although detecting the take can be difficult when the nymph needs to be sunk a few inches. It is surprising how a large fish can move quite suddenly under water without making an obvious disturbance on the surface.

The other main difference between the nymph and the dry fly is estimating the speed of the current, so that the nymph sinks to the fish's depth at the same time as it reaches the right spot. As with the dry fly, it is important to remember that a fish frequently lies some distance upstream of its rising position, and that it takes a few moments for the fish to adjust its position and inspect a fly before it takes it. This means, particularly in fast-flowing water, that the fish will often be lying more than a yard above the place where the surface has been disturbed by the rise.

Because the angler can also be fooled by refraction, it is easy to spend a great deal of time casting to a fish and not covering it properly. Once, when I was fishing with a friend, he was casting to a particularly difficult fish that was nymphing in about twelve inches of water beside some bridge pilings. From the only suitable casting position it was impossible for the angler to see the fish in the water sufficiently clearly to tell if his nymph had been taken.

I moved to a point alongside the fish but out of its sight, so that I could warn him when the nymph was taken. His first casts fell nearly a yard short, and I needed to be very reassuring in order to persuade him to lengthen his line sufficiently to cover the fish. He was convinced that the main fly line would land across the fish's lie if he extended any farther. He eventually covered the fish properly and hooked it.

When we discussed the problem afterwards, he said he was convinced that he frequently failed to rise fish simply because he was not covering them, and I am sure it is a problem a lot of anglers have, whether fishing a nymph or a dry fly. The solution is to begin casting to the place where you think the fish is lying and, if you get no response, gradually to lengthen line until you are sure you have covered the fish. The average leader is nine feet long, which gives you quite a large margin for error before you risk lining the fish.

When fishing a deep nymph it is essential to strike very quickly, because of the water resistance on the line and leader, but with Skues nymphs it is necessary to delay a little before setting the hook. This delay should not be as long as the delay for a dry fly. For some reason fish eject an artificial nymph much faster than they do a dry fly, but even so there must be some delay in setting the hook, particularly if the fish has had to turn upwards to intercept it. Hooking fish with Skues pattern nymphs is always a risky business and I have found that more fish come off with this kind of fly than with any other.

If you can see the fish in the water, it is best to delay the strike until you actually see that the leader has been arrested—rather than striking as soon as you see the fish's mouth close on the fly. Sawyer recommends setting the hook instantly when using his patterns. There is no question that detecting the take of a Skues nymph is usually relatively easy because, even if you cannot see the fish, there is a good length of leader floating on the surface, which acts as a bite detector. However, there are occasions, as I mentioned previously, when sixth sense takes over and the angler tightens automatically even though there is no obvious indication that his fly has been taken.

You will have noticed that I frequently refer to the use of the small hare's fur nymph for difficult fish. This is a fly in which I have gradually gained confidence over the years. Any really difficult fish will often take this nymph when it will look at no other artificial.

The whole question of having confidence in a fly is a fascinating one. Do you cast better to a rising fish when you believe you have chosen the right fly—or did the fish take that fly because it was the right one?

This is a problem worth considering because it can make a significant difference to the number of fish caught. Most of us, over a long period, develop the patterns we carry in our fly boxes as a direct result of success. We reject patterns that do not appear to work for us. But the interesting thing is that a fellow fisherman of similar ability will often take fish on a pattern we have rejected.

As you know, I tie my own flies, and I have a friend who does the same. However, we disagree vehemently over choices of colour and body material. I cannot catch fish with the flies he ties if that pattern does not have similar materials to those I choose.

The crucial question, therefore, is one of confidence. Do I fail to catch fish with his patterns because I have no confidence in them? Do I cast differently with one of his flies? Is there some subtle difference in presentation which makes him catch fish with that fly when I cannot?

The same thing works in reverse. He cannot catch fish with some of my flies. There are patterns which we do have in common, and we can happily exchange these and catch fish with them. I suspect that the real solution is perseverance. If you do not have confidence in a particular pattern you may use it for a while, but you will not stick with it if it seems unattractive.

I have four basic patterns of dry fly which I would never be without. These are Skues' little red sedge; my own tying of the medium olive with a dyed heron-herl body; a pheasant-tail spinner and the Skues dark hare's fur nymph. There are other patterns that I would choose to carry as well, but the four above are those I regard as essential. However, ask another dry fly man to make a selection of just four flies, and you can bet his choice will be different altogether. In my experience my four flies have proved more deadly in general circumstances than any other patterns, but I am sure they would not necessarily work for somebody else.

The next thing to study, therefore, is why any one individual should be completely besotted with a particular pattern. Why has it caught fish for him when it has let other people down? Strangely enough, I do not think this always depends on a pattern's particular fish-catching ability. There are some artificial flies whose appearance I like on the water. They seem to sit right—they cock properly and stand up. Some seem to cast better than others, or to land more lightly. Others seem easier to cast into a wind, and others seem perfectly to match the colour and attitude of the natural.

This question of confidence, it seems, is not based purely on blind prejudice, nor does it stem from having brought up a difficult fish on one occasion. The fish-catching ability almost seems a secondary consideration—first it seems necessary, for a variety of reasons, for the fisherman to like the fly. If it looks right and is fished often enough in the right circumstances, it will take fish.

But it goes even farther than this. My fly-tying friend has a particular preference for quill-bodied flies, whereas I much prefer the look of herl bodies. The quill body, admittedly, gives a particularly good striated effect, but to me seems to lack natural sparkle and translucence. Herl seems to have a depth to it and looks soft and tempting. I add the stripes with a rib of gold wire. Because I usually fish herl-bodied flies, I have more confidence in them.

I said that fishing a particular fly frequently enough bestows its user with confidence, and this is part of the problem when separating prejudice from a proper test based on experience. If your fly is on the water for long enough, the chances are that it will take more fish than one used less frequently, regardless of its attractiveness. The important thing is to fish the fly that gives you the most confidence, but only under the right circumstances. There is no point in fishing a little red sedge, for instance, to a fish that is obviously taking pale watery duns.

If you do not tie your own flies, there will still be certain patterns in tackle shops that appeal to you. When you fish these, you will establish preferences. It is wise to be guided by these preferences, but always remember that a fly that catches fish on one occasion is not necessarily infallible in all circumstances. After all, if it were, you would only need to carry one pattern.

The best way to form an opinion, even if your knowledge of entomology is shaky, is to find a pattern in your fly box that looks as near an imitation as possible to the natural fly on the water. Having done this and having caught a fish, put it to the same test on several occasions. If the fly consistently catches fish, you have found a pattern in which you can have confidence.

There will be occasions when you can see fish in the water which look as though they would be tempted, but because of the lack of fly they are not rising. Very often, in these circumstances, a sedge pattern will bring up a fish, and by trial and error it is possible to establish which of the sedge patterns you carry is the best.

The years 1989 and 1990 were exceptionally dry, with long, hot summers producing strong light and low, clear water which made dry fly fishing particularly difficult. Even fish approached with paranoid caution seemed to shoot into their hidy-holes as soon as line was lengthened to cover them.

This particular bashfulness on the part of the trout also extended to 'gut shyness'. This symptom is bad enough in educated trout on any fishery—particularly towards the end of the season when the 'old stagers' have seen more fishing rods than they have medium olives—but in low, clear water conditions it really becomes a problem.

I have come to the conclusion that far too many dry fly people fish much too coarse a point. Even waters stocked with huge trout (and even these big naive fish soon become sensitive to coarse nylon) do not require the strength of point used by many anglers. You will find very few fishermen beside the river who are fishing with a point of two pounds breaking strain or less.

It is an indication of fishing demand that few tackle manufacturers sell leaders going down to less than two pounds (6X or .005 inches), and many dry fly men would not dream of fishing even this fine, for fear of being broken; yet I am sure that in many cases flies are refused not because they are the wrong pattern or presented badly, but because the fish can see the nylon.

It is an interesting experiment to thread up a rod and attach a spring balance to the point of the leader. Get someone to apply as much leverage as he or she can to the butt of the rod so that it is fully deflected, and then see the maximum reading that can be obtained on the spring balance. With an average eight-and-a-half foot dry fly rod it is unlikely that even the strongest wrist, applied to the stiffest action rod, will exert more than a three pound reading on the scale.

What I am getting at, therefore, is that even the most safety-conscious fisherman need not fish with a point stronger than three pounds unless he is using mayflies or very large sedges, where additional stiffness in the leader is needed to help turn the point over and to resist the inevitable wear on the point caused by a heavy fly with a high wind resistance.

Anyone with a modicum of finesse should be able to handle a fish of at least three pounds on a point of no more than two pounds, providing the water is not riddled with snags. It is worth remembering two significant rules when fighting a fish. The first is that even a fish weighing more than three pounds is unlikely to be able to exert all its body weight against the strength of the point and, second, that the cushioning effect of an upraised rod will dampen the worst shocks from a plunging fish.

If you play your fish properly, with the full action of the rod being used to cushion the movement of the fish, and discreet use of the reel allowing line to be given during a headlong rush, there is no reason why a fish weighing more than twice the nominal breaking strain of the leader should break you.

The only time you are likely to meet trouble is with snags and weed—but even in these circumstances the judicious use of side strain to steer your fish away from trouble will normally save the day.

It must be remembered that a fish can effectively increase its weight by using the strength of the current to its advantage. It is vital, therefore, not to allow the fish to get downstream of you.

There has also been the recent development of braided leaders which are made to take tippets of varying diameter. The tippet is the finest point of the leader and can be changeable either to change the breaking strain of the leader or to lengthen and shorten it. During last season I tried one of these new leaders and have been delighted with its performance. I do not bother to use the tippets supplied by the leader maker, but simply use my own Drennan double-strength monofilament as the tippet. This is attached to a coarser length of nylon which in turn is attached to the braided leader. Each of the connections is made with simple loop-to-loop joints which are quick to attach and detach, making them easy to change in poor light.

If you are against braided leaders it is best to buy conventional 5X traces and chop off the bottom twelve inches or so, which you can then replace with parallel monofilament of suitable fineness.

It is also worth remembering that when using a continuous tapered leader, every time you change your fly you are losing at least a few inches of the point, so that the tip diameter is increasing each time. It would be interesting to take a micrometer to the point of the average fisherman's leader at the end of a day's fishing. I can guarantee you will find plenty who are fishing with a point approaching .010 inches, which is roughly equivalent to a breaking strain of seven pounds! Is it any wonder that so many anglers complain that they are having difficulty tempting fish during an evening rise?

Perhaps it is wise to offer a little advice on precautions that should be taken when fishing very fine. Probably the most common time to be broken by a fish is on the strike. Very often all the pent-up excitement of finally persuading a trout to take your fly is released in the strike. As the fish is turning down to resume its position, the angler raises the rod tip to drive the point of the hook home. Frequently this is done with far too much enthusiasm. Only two things can happen: either the fish will be dragged backwards through the water, or the point will break.

The fisherman must learn to suppress his enthusiasm, and simply give a sharp turn of wrist to flick the rod tip upwards, which sets the hook firmly. Obviously the length of the line between the angler and his quarry will have a considerable bearing on the amount of effort required to set the hook. In these circumstances there are two considerations and unfortunately they are conflicting ones.

In order to time the strike accurately, more pace needs to be imparted to the line when striking a fish at some distance. More pace effectively means more weight, with the result that the force of the strike increases with additional line speed. But if the hook is to be set before the trout spits out the fly, considerable speed is needed to transmit the movement of the rod tip down the length of line and leader to the hook. This problem is exacerbated by a tapered fly line. The more line that is out, the more it weighs, and because of the taper this is a compound progression. The problem requires fine judgement, but it is worth remembering that you usually have much more time than you think when fishing a dry fly. It takes a trout several moments to decide that what it thought was a tasty morsel is no more than a bunch of fur and feather.

Having hooked your trout, the next problem is to play it. When fishing fine it is obvious that more delicacy is needed than when you have the security of a thick leader, but there is far more satisfaction if you have to outwit your fish after hooking it as well as before! When hooked, trout normally do one of two things—they either make a dash for their bolt-hole, which is usually nearby, or they will jump.

Immediately after hooking a fish the angler has the advantage of surprise. The fish is not aware of what has happened to it and is usually off balance, so a judicious tug in the right direction will normally steer it out towards clear water where it can be played in relative safety.

Hooked trout will frequently use the resistance of the line as a lever to propel them out of the water, so remember to handle the fish gently, using progressive pressure to manoeuvre it where you want it. It is best to play a fish by steering it, rather than simply wrestling with it.

I know this all sounds very simple in theory, when in fact the rush and dash of a struggling trout is at times very difficult to read and very difficult to control on a fine point. In the final analysis, I would rather stand a chance of rising a fish on a fine point and risk the occasional loss than not rise it at all because it has spotted my leader.

NM '90

Chapter Nine

Most of my fishing experience has been on southern rivers, but after first learning to cast a fly I use to make regular trips to Brecon to fish the day ticket water on the Usk, just downstream of the bridge. It was here that I saw a significant hatch of fly for the first time.

At one point I was flogging away on the water, fishing a wet fly downstream, wondering if there were any fish in the river. A moment later fish started to rise all over the water. I was kneeling on a rock at the time, a few feet above the water's surface. A fish rose just near me and I peered down into the river. I saw a largish drab brown fly emerge on the surface, flexing its wings and struggling to retain its balance. At that moment there was a swirl as a trout's nose broke the surface and snatched the fly.

I knew very little about dry fly fishing at this stage, but it was obvious even to my meagre intellect that if I were to catch one of these trout I would have to offer it a copy of a fly similar to the one I had just seen swallowed.

All the patterns in my box were wet flies, but there was one brown bushy specimen that might float. I tied on the fly with shaking hands and cast to the place where the trout had risen. Despite repeated casts the fish did not rise, and after what seemed only a few minutes the hatch was over and the river returned to its dead state.

I later learned that I had witnessed a hatch of March browns, but the incident made me appreciate the difference between wet and dry flies, when fished in the right circumstances. I continued visiting the Usk and other Welsh rivers after I had gained some dry fly fishing knowledge in southern England, and I began to build some experience of fishing the dry fly on rain-fed streams.

I think perhaps my Usk experience with the March brown probably coloured my view of wet fly fishing. When fishing the wet fly I only caught very small trout or salmon parr, but I had witnessed a good-sized trout taking a dry fly and this helped to determine the way I was to fish for the rest of my life. I believed that the best trout would be caught on the dry fly and I was surprised that the native fishermen of Wales had not cottoned on to what they were missing. They fished wet flies almost exclusively!

Although it took me some time to realise that the best way to catch trout on the Welsh, Scottish and West Country rivers is generally with a wet fly, it does still surprise me sometimes that dry flies are not used more often when conditions suit this method of fishing. I have learned, of course, that my early wet fly fishing was largely doomed to failure through my own lack of skill and experience, but there is no question that there is room for the dry fly on any water that holds trout.

Because of my love of the dry fly and nymph, I fish them exclusively wherever I go. The tactics for fishing dry flies on fast rocky streams are considerably different from those needed on the relative placidness of the southern chalk streams. Quite a lot of the Usk is slow-flowing and is fringed with trees, under which it is possible to find fish lying ready to take anything that looks like food.

Dry fly fishing on rain-fed rivers is a matter not so much of stalking rising fish as of using the fly to search the pools, glides and eddies. Even fast stickles can be fished with a bushy, well-oiled fly, which will resist being drowned in the turbulence. The fish in this fast water are usually small and take the fly very fast. On occasion it is difficult to see if the fly has been taken as it bounces over the rough water, and under these circumstances it is a good fisherman who can average hooking one fish in three.

The dry fly really comes into its own on the glassy glides above rapids. Even the naive fish of rain-fed rivers are hard to fool where the water is clear and undisturbed by ripples. The tell-tale wake left by a dragging wet fly is enough to make even the smallest fish dash for cover. The innocent-looking dry fly, if it can be fished without drag, will usually bring up the larger fish when cast accurately.

Through a Welsh friend I was fortunate to get some fishing on the river Teifi, not far from Lampeter. There was one particular pool that was deep and clear, and good-sized trout were lying in the depths. These were educated fish which had seen many a wet fly. I tried them first with a weighted nymph, but they completely ignored it. Although the fish were lying in about ten feet of water, I decided to try a large floating sedge that would be carried across the pool by the current. I caught three trout, each weighing about a pound.

When the fish saw the fly they shot up to the surface and grabbed it. Two of them hooked themselves as they turned downwards to regain their lie in the depths of the pool. The tumult caused by landing the three fish scared the others, but I took another two the following day, using the same technique.

On another section of the same river the main current flowed under some trees growing on the far bank. The water was quite rough from the current and it was impossible to see if there were any fish lying there, although it looked very 'trouty'. In a stretch of less than a hundred yards I must have risen twenty fish to a small blue dun, although I only hooked and landed four of them. The best probably weighed about half a pound, but the fishing was really good fun. All the fish I caught on the Teifi fought gamely, far out of proportion to their size. None was fussy about the fly pattern and there were no visible natural flies on the water.

On the farm where I was fishing there was a deep eddy where the current rounded a rock and had scoured out the muddy bank behind it. The water was not so clear in this pool and I could not see any fish, but I decided to give it a try. My small sedge was still in the air over the water when a fish of about twelve ounces leapt at it and hooked itself. I caught and returned five fish in this pool.

I spent two days fishing the Teifi, and although I never caught a fish over one-and-a-half pounds, I had one of the most enjoyable fishing weekends I can remember. I keep promising myself I shall go back.

A few years ago a friend of mine was going to Scotland on business for several days, and asked me if I would keep him company. His destination was Kinross, not far north of Edinburgh. After booking into a hotel we went for a look round. We walked down to Loch Leven and took a boat across to Queen Mary's Castle. In the lee of the castle the surface of the water was thick with midges. Fish were swimming within a few yards of the boat, gobbling up the little black flies. I was tempted to fish Loch Leven, even though still water is not my favourite sort of fishing.

Back at the hotel I made enquiries, but when I discovered the price of fishing and boat hire I decided against the loch; I discovered, however, that there was supposed to be reasonable trout fishing on the river Devon, a small stream that runs through the appropriately named Rumblingbridge on its journey to the river Forth.

I was told I could buy a permit at Rumblingbridge Post Office, so the following day I set off to get my ticket. It was early in September and the weather was warm and sunny, as it so often is during early autumn in Scotland. I entered the post office and found myself in a tiny room, one wall of which was almost completely taken over by an enormous fireplace containing a roaring fire.

An elderly lady behind the counter enquired what I wanted. She had some difficulty understanding my English but I eventually managed to make myself clear. My permit, she said, would be 'half-a-croon'. This was several years after decimalisation.

It turned out that I had the run of several miles of one of the most beautiful rivers I have ever seen. The Devon has wide, flat runs, deep, plunging gorges and a series of fast stickles over a shale bottom.

My best approach to the river was along a railway line. The area was heavily wooded, with large beech trees growing down to the water's edge. Because of the wooded nature of the banks, wading would be essential. I climbed down over some rocks and waded out into the river. It was like entering a green cathedral. The columns of the beech trees arched up to a viridian canopy so green that the whole river was bright with the awe-inspiring tinted light.

I had walked into another world. The water was no more than two feet deep and gurgled and splashed as it ran over rocks and shale. There was a larger rock sticking out of the water some fifteen or twenty feet upstream of me. The water ran round its edges and this was where I placed my first cast. As the fly charged round the turbulence at the rock's edge there was a splash. I tightened and was into my first Scottish trout. After a brief fight I had a fish of about ten inches at my feet. I ran my hand down the trace, caught the fly and shook the fish off.

I cast to the other side of the rock after re-oiling the fly, and rose but missed another fish. I cast again and rose the fish again, but still failed to make contact. This happened once more and for a moment I thought I must have lost the hook point, but an inspection showed that it was still intact.

The beech-vaulted section of river must have extended for nearly two hundred yards, and I fished it slowly all the way up, casting to any swirl or eddy that looked as though it could hold a fish. I lost count of the number of missed fish and of those I shook off. Most of them measured between six and twelve inches and were all beautifully marked with red and black spots, with an iridescent deep blue panel running the length of their bodies each side of the lateral line. Their backs were nearly black and their bellies pure white.

After spending my morning in the 'cathedral', I decided to explore downstream. There was a worn path along much of the bank, although for the three days I fished this river I never saw another soul. After flowing out of the beeches the river plunged through a series of steep rapids as it descended into an ever deepening gorge. The volume of water pouring through the narrow rapids made it impossible to fish with a dry fly, but I continued to scramble down-stream over the slippery rocks.

The river opened out a little and the far bank of steep rocky cliffs gradually eased back, leaving a wide plateau on which stood a beautiful stone cottage. What a place to live! I never quite managed to work out the geography of the river valley, otherwise I would have attempted to find the house by road, just to see how the residents got there.

Downstream of the house the river ran into a series of deep pools linked by fast, tumbling narrows. Perched on the rocks above the pools I cast my fly across the river, searching the shallower water. Occasionally I rose and hooked a fish of similar size to those in the 'cathedral', but this was not ideal water for the dry fly; it really needed a sinking line or a crafty worm.

The local businessmen who drank in the hotel bar in the evening were a friendly and helpful lot. They said that occasional sea trout and salmon got up as far as Rumblingbridge, but otherwise the trout mostly only weighed about eight ounces, although there had been two-pounders taken from the river. During my three days my best fish probably weighed just under a pound, but in those idyllic surroundings any fish were a bonus and there was no shortage of them.

I returned to Scotland some years later, on holiday with my family. My boys were both keen to have fly fishing lessons and we spent many happy hours fishing some of the streams that flowed into Loch Ness. The trout were very small, but they were keen to rise to any artificial pattern that alighted on the surface of the river. It was the ideal place for children to learn the basics of fly fishing because they could catch fish almost from the first cast.

In the evenings I took to making outings up some of the streams by myself. I would use a dry fly to search any pockets under trees along the banks. None of the fish I caught was big but it was fun to search out the difficult nooks and crannies along the banks and most casts produced a rise.

My love of the dry fly has precluded me from taking an interest in fishing for sea trout or salmon, but I have heard that sea trout will sometimes be persuaded to take a moth pattern fished on the surface. It has now been some years since I have fished either in Wales or Scotland, but I must admit I am tempted to organise a trip to try sea trout on the dry fly.

The Gloucestershire Coln is a delightful river in the Cotswolds, which flows into the Thames near Lechlade. Somebody once gave me an out-of-date edition of *Where to Fish* published by *The Field*. In this there was a picture of the Coln which prompted me to make some telephone calls to try for some fishing on this lovely-looking river.

Day tickets were available from the Bull Hotel at Fairford. I booked two rods during the mayfly season for a friend and myself. The water was well stocked with trout and also had a native population of grayling, some of which were huge. There was about one-and-a-half miles of water flowing round the hotel's vegetable garden and out across farm meadows. On our first visit we both caught two or three fish and for several years the Coln became an annual mayfly pilgrimage.

The lower end of the water was quite deep and slow-flowing and there were occasional large trout which rose to mayfly duns during the afternoon and to spinners in the evening. The fish were difficult to tempt and the wind on this section of the water was often troublesome. On one occasion I hooked a really good trout that plunged into some roots and broke me.

A little higher up, the water was broken into pools and fast runs. Trout and grayling rose regularly in these pools, but they were fussy over mayfly patterns and were by no means easy to fool. On various outings I caught several fish here, and also lost several among the reeds that lined the banks.

Perhaps the best of the fishing was from the banks of the open meadows. The river was quite wide, with prolific growths of ranunculus. Fish lay in the runs between the banks of weed, sucking in mayflies as they passed over the lies. As so often happens in May, there were strong winds from the east, which frequently gusted down this open part of the river. The hatching duns would tumble over the surface and fish would charge across considerable distances to capture the flies before they took off.

The best of the grayling lay in a pool just below the hotel kitchen garden. Their large blue-grey shadows would lurk in the deeps and could only occasionally be tempted with a dry fly. Nymph fishing was banned in those days, which was unfortunate because I am sure those big grayling would have been more easily tempted with a sunk fly.

My best grayling from there weighed over two pounds and was taken on a mayfly dun. I never caught a native trout from the Coln;

they all seemed to be stockies and averaged about one-and-a-half pounds.

The vegetable garden was on an island formed by the main river on one side and a small stream on the other. Quite large trout could be seen in the stream and I spent many absorbing hours in cramped conditions under bushes and saplings, trying to cover these fish. Few mayflies hatched in the stream, but medium olives were plentiful and I spent some time one morning casting to a trout that lay in a shallow pool below a small footbridge. The breeze was contrary and inconsistent as it blew round the side of a small barn and stable block on the mainland side of the stream.

The fish was not prepared to take a fly that passed more than about three inches away from its lie. After some time the fly landed accurately and passed right over the fish. I saw its head come up and the trout followed the fly with its nose almost resting against its underside. At the last moment it opened its mouth in a leisurely fashion. As its head went down I tightened gently. The fish shot up under the bridge and I could see my leader and the line chaffing against the timbers. I dropped the rod sideways and applied as much pressure as I could, but the trout resisted.

The fish must have pulled nearly twenty yards of line off the reel with its first rush before I could turn it. It tried to get into reeds growing close to the far bank above the bridge, but eventually it turned back under the bridge and I was convinced I had it beaten as it came back towards me. As soon as the fish saw me it kicked again, this time shooting off downstream. I began to wonder if it was foul hooked, caught by a part of its body other than the mouth, because it wasn't all that big and yet it seemed virtually unstoppable.

I was still worried about being broken, particularly as the trout was now downstream of me and could use the weight of the current to its advantage. I set off in pursuit, reeling in as I ran. I had to pass my rod round the trunks of several saplings before I could get back on equal terms. The bank was quite high, so that when I finally had the fish subdued I still needed to find a suitable place to net it out. There was a small open space where watercress grew. I stumbled into this, sinking into mud up to my knees. The fish bolted again as I extended the net under it, but it was beaten now and I eventually managed to draw it over the net and lift it clear of the water.

It was a trout of one pound fourteen ounces and was hooked exactly in the point of its nose. I remembered reading in one of Skues' books that fish hooked in the nose fought much harder than those hooked elsewhere in the mouth. Since then I have caught one or two others that have been hooked in the same place and they have always been much more difficult to subdue than their size would suggest.

The year after that was to be my last outing to the Coln. The river and the mayfly hatch were a real disappointment that year; I saw no trout in the water and the few mayfly that floated down on the stream were ignored. A new estate had been built not far from the riverside meadows, and during the day several people walked their dogs along the river and threw sticks in the water for the dogs to retrieve. The owners were deaf to protestations about spoiling the fishing. I have often thought about the river since and have toyed with the idea of trying to find somewhere less public, which issues day tickets during the mayfly season, but I suspect that the rest of the river is well preserved for season rods or syndicates.

My most recent visit to Wales was made when my younger son, James, was offered a choice of holiday venues and asked if we could stay in Llangammarch Wells on the river Irfon. He was keen to do more fly fishing and we booked in at the Lake Hotel, which offered fishing both on the river and on a lake in the hotel grounds.

The river formed part of the boundary for the hotel grounds and we spent a lot of time fishing for small trout and huge chub. The water was low and it was possible to wade across the shallows. My son had grown tired of fishing a fly and was using a coarse fishing rod to trot worms through some of the faster water. I climbed a bank downstream of him and saw a large salmon resting in a shallow pool below the point where James was fishing. I told him to lengthen his line to reach the salmon. I was perched in some bushes above the fish and saw it turn towards the bait three or four times, but every time it shied away at the last minute.

After a while the salmon became bored with the game and sank out of sight into deeper water, but a school of chub made their way up one side of the pool and James caught two of them. Both must have weighed over three pounds, but surprisingly neither gave much of a fight. Later in the day I took my fly rod upstream to a place where there were supposed to be some good trout. In a deep pool below my own bank I saw a shoal of chub that were circulating near the surface. I put on a large sedge pattern and cast to the largest chub in the group. As the fly landed on the surface the chub moved towards it and nosed the fly. I gave it a slight twitch and the fish's large, lazy mouth closed on the sedge. As I set the hook the water erupted and the chub shot out into the main current, scattering the rest of the shoal as it went. The fight was limited to the first rush, but it was quite exciting on a fly rod and 5X leader.

After a short pause the shoal returned to the pool and I chose another fish and dropped the fly in front of it. In the space of the next hour or so I caught five chub, all weighing around the four pound mark. They all fought the same way, making an initial rush and then allowing themselves to be reeled in and netted out without resistance.

After this I went looking for the fabled two pound trout which I had been told about at the hotel. There was one place where the river flowed between two wide, flat beds of rock. The river was narrow and deep and very dark at this point. The gloom was caused by trees that met overhead, growing from the high banks behind. The flat beds of rock, I suspect, normally formed a shallow plateau in the river bed but, because of the low water, the flow was restricted to a dark narrow stream below this level.

By this time it was early evening and I hoped that there might be a hatch of sedges or some other fly that would bring up some decent-sized trout. I stood at the downstream end of the rock plateau and waited for something to happen. After a while I began to notice disturbances in the surface of the gurgling gully. The rises were by no means easy to spot, partly because of the gloom and partly because the surface was quite agitated.

I moved up, preparing to cast to the nearest fish. I could see no fly on the water, but decided that a small sedge would be the best bet. The small trout that I had previously caught lower down certainly did not seem to be fussy over fly patterns. As soon as I covered the nearest fish it stopped rising and the same thing happened every time I moved up and covered another.

I tied on a small pale evening dun, but still the fish went down as soon as I covered them. The fish below me had started to rise again, although there was still no fly visible on the surface, and I was perplexed. I decided to retrace my steps and start again with a small pheasant tail nymph fished just below the surface. My nymph dropped a couple of feet upstream of the nearest fish and I could just make out the leader as it swam down on the current. For some reason I decided to tighten and there was a splash. I was into a trout that fought like a mad thing for several minutes. I eventually netted out a beautiful fish of about fourteen ounces. Its flanks were dark greenish brown with bright red spots. The fins were a pinkish colour and its back was inky black.

I moved up to the next fish and rose it at once. It dived and I felt a dead resistance on the line. I pulled harder and my line came away minus the point, the fly and the fish. I had obviously been snagged on a rock. Nearly every cast produced a fish, with the best weighing nearly one-and-a-half pounds.

When it was too dark to see under the trees I moved upstream, out into the open. There were fish rising in a wide pool below the village bridge and I caught several of these, but they were all small. That gully seemed the only place that produced good-sized fish.

It was on another holiday, this time to north Devon, that I tried fishing the rain-fed rivers of the West Country. The beauty of the river Devon in Scotland was still fresh in my memory when I climbed the footpath beside the river Lyn, but the loveliness of the Water-smeet valley rivalled even the Scottish river. Beautiful deciduous trees plunged down rocky valleys to the water's edge. It was hard to believe that the dancing stream in the valley had been responsible for the deaths of many people in the Lynton and Lynmouth flood disaster of the early 1950s.

Because of family commitments I only spent one evening fishing the Lyn in the Watersmeet valley. I watched a dogged sea trout of about three pounds attempting to climb one waterfall, but after many attempts the fish dropped back exhausted into the pool below. There were other sea trout in the pool, but they were all lying deep, perhaps waiting for a spate to ease their way upstream.

Because of the trees so close to the water, in most places it was only possible to fish while wading. I caught several small trout on a dry fly, but I was disappointed not to see or catch anything of decent size.

The water looked very promising and there were numerous rises under the trees and in the rocky pools and eddies.

We rented a cottage on a farm just outside Lynton where there was a small stream flowing within a few yards of the front door. I caught dozens of trout up to eight inches long from this stream, which was no deeper than eighteen inches in most places. Despite the lack of good-sized fish, the scenery more than made up for the poor fishing. It was a delight just to be out in the countryside.

Chapter Ten

There is a golden tinge in the water meadows, the bankside balsam glows like a dying fire and the odd dead leaf spins in small eddies on the chalk stream. It is September, the beginning of autumn, and even the trout have taken on a golden hue.

Fish will rise at this time of year as at no other. Gone is the spring feeding frenzy and the sultriness of summer, to be replaced by a steady rise as if the fish know that this is their last chance to put on weight before the exhausting effort of spawning and the winter dearth of food.

The medium olive is back on the water in droves during the day, although the autumn fly is somewhat smaller and paler than its spring cousin. Quite often the evening will be warm enough to produce a hatch of blue winged olives, and there are still pale wateries and spurwings hatching.

While the trout fisherman has a touch of melancholy about him—knowing that his season is fast drawing to a close—he still has that feeling of anticipation. He knows that September will provide an opportunity to tempt large fish which have evaded him all season.

The huge trout that lives in the depths of a dark sluice could well be seduced by an evening daddy-long-legs or grass moth. The leviathon which, all summer, has sheltered under cool roots on the main river, feeding on fry, knows that he too must put on weight if he is to survive the rigours of winter. A big late evening sedge should even tempt him to rise at this time of year.

But be warned: although trout seem to rise more readily in September than in any other month, they have also had a season's education into the wiles of the man who stands on the bank with a fishing rod in his hand. The particular diffused light of a sunny day in autumn combines with low, clear water to provide trout with a quality of vision that makes them desperately difficult to approach.

Flies hatch earlier in September than at most other times, and the angler should be on the water by 10.30 a.m. Usually the medium olives are the first to start drifting down on the current. It is often not until after noon that the first of the pale wateries will appear, and despite the still conditions frequently spurned in the spring by the iron blue, this fly will sometimes put in an appearance during the afternoon.

Quite frequently there will be black gnat on the water all day long. This is a fly much harder to imitate than its reputation suggests. There are frequently very small examples on the water, which are taken greedily by the trout. If you buy flies rather than making them yourself, it is a good idea to buy several in the smallest size available and tied as sparsely as possible—in September size 16 is the largest size normally useful, and 18 is better if you can get it.

If you are to rise these wary fish a fine point is essential. Despite the heavier average weight of fish at this time of year, I would advocate a leader point of no more two pounds breaking strain (approx. 005 inches). It is surprising how much effort can be exerted on a fish when using a two pound point, but remember that it is vital to keep the fish upstream of you when playing it. A trout's body weight is effectively increased considerably when it has its flank exposed to the force of the current.

There is another feature of September trout. More of them will be found lying under the banks than is usual at other times of year, so that rises are usually more delicate and hard to spot. It is important to keep a close eye under your own bank. Frequently rises will be heard before they are seen, so keep your ears open, too. A quiet sip will often betray a large fish lying in ridiculously shallow water below bankside vegetation.

One advantage with fish lying in this position is that it is possible to get closer to them than to those lying out in clear water, because much of their vision is impeded by the growth on the banks. The disadvantage is that very accurate casting is needed, with the angler often having to flirt with the dangers of the bankside growth. These trout feeding under banks are not prepared to move more than a few inches to intercept a fly, so the artificial must be dropped precisely.

Once hooked, the fish should be hustled out into open water away from bankside snags. Even when you have hooked a fish it is best to keep out of sight. Trout do not take nearly so much fright if they cannot see what is restraining them, and the task of controlling them is made much easier at close quarters. It is best to put your landing net in the water, with the handle resting on the bank, before drawing the fish towards you. This avoids additional fright which could lead to the trout making another dash for freedom if it sees a net plunged into the water in front of it.

One of the problems associated with September fishing on rivers which are heavily stocked is the early pairing of cocks and hens. When trout start to pair up in preparation for spawning they tend to mill and chase around the water and are impossible to tempt with a fly.

For some reason stockies seem to pair up much earlier than fish native to the river. It has been argued that this has been caused by fish farmers who have tended to breed from trout that are ripe earlier in the year. As this has gone on from season to season, the natural spawning instincts of the fish have been brought forward in the calendar.

Whatever the cause, it is a nuisance and tends to make the autumn angler feel guilty at being by the riverside. There have been several years when I have stopped fishing some weeks before the official end to the season.

Nowadays pressures of work are such that I rarely have time to spend a full day beside my beloved River Itchen during the season, but I still dread the coming of 1st October, knowing that I shall not be able to cast a fly for more than six months.

I know a number of fishermen who effectively extend their season by going grayling fishing in the autumn and winter. While I have no objection to grayling, my first love is catching trout and I have never done any fishing specifically for grayling, although those who do tell me that it is an art in itself.

My first thoughts at the end of the season are that this winter I really will sit down and tie all the flies I need for next year. Every year I also say to myself that this winter I shall have a blitz on my fly-tying chest. I shall sort out all the wing feathers, all the hackles, all the silks, all the pheasant tails and the huge quantity of furs and wools that I have amassed, and I shall catalogue them according to colour, size, shape and use and file them away in clearly marked boxes so that I can find them instantly when I want them.

I am sure I don't have to tell you that I have never done this, nor have I ever started a fishing season with a full complement of flies. To be fair, I do write quite a bit in the winter and I do tie some flies, but the flies tied in the winter never seem to be exactly what I want the following season.

There is no question that the same species of fly does seem to vary slightly in size and colour from one season to the other. They also seem to vary very considerably in importance. A few seasons ago, for instance, there were hardly any decent hatches of medium olive on my water. I normally look upon the medium olive as the trout's staple fly, and the contents of my fly box usually reflect that. But at the end of that season I still had many medium olives in my fly box virtually untouched.

This can mean that it is generally better to tie flies as the season progresses. When you have seen what is attracting fish, you can tie some up for next time, and you can tie them in the size and colour that you have seen on the water.

Having told you what I don't do in the winter, perhaps I had better tell you what I do. I have a particular weakness that I call 'bridge gazing'. I can spend hours flirting with traffic in narrow country lanes, leaning over bridges and gazing into the water below. My friend Bob Schröder has a similar disposition, so when I have some time off I telephone him and we go out bridge-prospecting. We can both spend hours gazing into rivers, speculating on their trout population and quality, and generally making observations about the merits or otherwise of the particular beats we are studying.

We have done this in the freezing cold and pouring rain, but have still thoroughly enjoyed ourselves. What is it about another person's water that always makes it look better than yours? Why can you always spot fish that are lying in the perfect position to be reached with a simple cast? What is it about the shape of a particular bend that makes it so muc.. better for holding fish than the bends on your own river? And even worse, why is it that the season is long over and yet there are fish rising all over the river? It is all so frustrating and fascinating.

We usually start our winter pilgrimage on the upper Itchen, just below Alresford. The back road from Alresford to Kingsworthy, with a few minor diversions, has a feast of bridges. The first is just a few hundred yards from the Alresford junction and they offer more and more splendid vistas from then on. Take a look at the map—it is really worth a visit.

We usually travel as far as Winchester before turning on to the Stockbridge road and going over to the Test. After a fortifying pint of beer in Stockbridge, we wander down the High Street and gaze over the bridge at the bottom of the town. After this there is a decision to be made: do we go upstream towards Leckford, or downstream to Romsey, or do we go across country to the Avon with its mighty bridges and deep, swift water?

While on the subject of winter, fishermen can only hope that the trend towards drier winters will not continue. Despite the cost, all of us as water consumers are going to have to face the fact that if we do not want our heritage of rivers destroyed, something will have to be done to reduce the amount of water abstraction at source. One long-term solution may be to abstract water at river mouths. This will involve a lot more cleaning and a complete re-think over pipe-work and purification processes, but unless it is done many of our most beautiful rivers and their indigenous wildlife may be lost for ever.

Abstraction at estuaries may cause us all to think again about pollution and what it costs. It seems madness to pump expensive poisonous chemicals onto the land, only to have to spend billions of pounds removing them at water treatment plants.

It is worth remembering that pollutants present in the water are less damaging if they are diluted, so the more water there is in the river, the less toxic the pollutants become. A greater rate of flow also produces more dissolved oxygen in the water, which in turn helps the river's self-cleaning properties.

The nonsenses over water management by statutory bodies are not the only threat to our rivers and their wildlife. In Chapter Seven I mentioned the fish-killing policy recently adopted by one fishing club on the Itchen, which in my view will lead to an ever-decreasing population of indigenous Itchen trout. This is not the only destructive rule or policy operated by riparian owners, clubs and syndicates on our rivers.

There is no question that, if there were no fishermen, our lakes and rivers would not be nearly so well guarded and nurtured. The price paid for this husbandry unfortunately means that many rivers are over-cultivated. They are stocked with fish that are much larger and more numerous than the water would naturally produce—but keepers cannot be blamed for this. They are normally only complying with the wishes of their members who demand large, naive fish that can be brought home like trophies to be paraded in front of the family. It is rare to hear a fisherman speak of the beauty of his catch. He usually only relates its size or weight.

I am also concerned about the amount of weed-cutting that takes place on some fisheries. One of the problems confronting fishery managers on the chalk streams is the agreement that is reached between riparian owners, clubs and syndicates over weed-cutting dates.

This agreement is necessary if anglers are to be able to go fishing, secure in the knowledge that their enjoyment is not going to be ruined by weed-cutting activities upstream of them. The result, unfortunately, is that on the agreed dates shortly before a period of anticipated heavy growth, the weed is often cut extremely severely.

Nobody knows how much damage is done to the sub-aqueous insect life as a result of cutting, but there is evidence that fly hatches on our chalk streams used to be considerably more frequent and abundant than they are today. Weed-cutting on the chalk streams has been carried out for a long time, but I suspect not with the intensity that it is today. There is no question that some of the depletion of insect stocks on the chalk streams has been caused by the indiscriminate use of agricultural chemicals, but I don't believe that these are entirely to blame.

It is only necessary to pull a handful of cut weed from the water and see the teeming life within it, to realise how many creatures are being washed downstream or dragged out onto the banks during weed-cutting sessions. It is also significant that on water where the weed is only cut lightly, or not at all, fly hatches seem to be more prolific.

I am not suggesting that weed-cutting should be stopped—it would make fishing on many waters almost impossible—but I do think that more research should be carried out into the effects of severe cutting.

I also have some disquiet about electro-fishing. This method is now adopted on most stretches of trout rivers in order to reduce stocks of coarse fish and grayling. It is argued that fly-life remains undamaged by electro-fishing because it is only the larger creatures in the water that have sufficient surface area exposed to the electrical current to be stunned by the charge. I think there is a case for more reasearch to be carried out into the effects of the current on aquatic insects.

One other aspect of fishery management applies to waterside wildlife. Although well-cut paths and banks may make life easier for the fisherman, they make life far harder for the varied mammals that live in the water meadows. Larger swathes of cut paths along the river banks leave a dangerously open desert for creatures to cross in order to gain access to the water. They are easily spotted by predators as they cross paths to find somewhere to drink and groom themselves.

My concept of the ideal fishery is a place where it is possible to fool myself that no one else has been. The sight of a discarded piece of paper or cigarette packet seems particularly offensive because it acts as a reminder of the presence of man. Neatly cut banks and bushes give me a similar feeling. It is hard to fool yourself that you are the only person there when you are surrounded by evidence of your fellows. This does not mean that I dislike company beside the river. Some people are a great pleasure to fish with, but there are occasions when one wishes to be alone, to enjoy the natural surroundings and gain pleasure from solitude.

Despite many years devising the best way to capture the creature, my affection for the trout and my fascination with it continue to grow. As one's ability in any sport improves, it often brings with it a certain cynicism and disdain. I find that the longer I fish for trout, the more respect I have for them and the more I want to find out about them.

The fascination I felt as a small boy, when I caught my first gudgeon from a muddy lake, is still with me. I may no longer fish with an old bamboo rod of doubtful reliability, nor do I use bread paste to lure my quarry, but I am still transfixed by the sight of a fish as it comes dancing from the water, and my feelings at having captured it are a mixture of awe and pity.

My fervent prayer is that I shall be able to continue fishing for the rest of my days. It gives a whole new meaning to the expression: 'He died with his boots on!'

Further Reading

A. Courtney Williams. *A Dictionary of Trout Flies.* A. & C. Black, 1949.

John Goddard. *Trout Fly Recognition.* A. & C. Black, 1966.

John Goddard and Brian Clarke. *The Trout and the Fly.* Ernest Benn, 1980.

G. E. M. Skues. *The Chalk Stream Angler.* Barry Shurlock, 1932.

Richard Walker. *Fly Dressing Innovations.* Ernest Benn, 1974.

Where to Fish, published annually by *The Field.*

OUR GOLF-FRIENDS:

Errol, the pro in our story. Has demi-god status in the club and is loved by everyone for his professional work, great advice, cool one-liners, amazing... you get the picture. He's the pro.

Dr. B.T. Jameson, infected by the golf virus for years now. The B.T. stands for Benjamin Thomas but once people get to know him, Big Talker seems to be more suitable. He's quite loose at the lips but otherwise means well. He just doesn't seem to understand how people don't share his point of view. Handicap? Regardless of what he says it's actually 20.

Benny, the coolest kid on the links and an excellent golfer to boot. Not always quite sure regarding golf etiquette but he's working on it. He finds golf, the club and Errol all cool and wouldn't mind becoming a pro himself one day... or maybe an astronaut, or movie star or president, or even...

Charles Beidebook. You guessed it, the name says it all. Lawyer and passionate golfer. Loves the game because of the strict rules. Spends every free minute on the golf course and usually alone at that. No wonder.

The lovely Claire! Sometimes has trouble distinguishing between golf time and tea time but loves the fresh air, the great people and works hard on improving her game. Handicap? What handicap?

This is our holy place. A place we all know very well. A place of relaxation, peace & quiet, many successes and not to mention, the place of our most bitter disappointments...
The Golf Club!

The place to meet many interesting people...

...and, oh well, unfortunately not so interesting...

Hey friend, you call that a shot? Don't worry, I have just the trick.

You're holding the club all wrong. I used to make the same mistake *once*. You have to change your grip.

A tip from the pro at Britannia Beach – maybe you've heard of it. It is thee top club in the whole US of A...

...where I, by the way, just happened to spend two weeks vacation again. Hey, hang on. Where ya'll goin?

Hey, there's Errol. I bet he'll be happy to see me again.

* A "mulligan" describes when a player is allowed to replay any one shot per hole.
Whereas no official evaluation is then possible afterwards.

7

* It is forbidden to borrow a club during play (2 penalty strokes)

** Outside the obstacle, not closer to hole

9

* Lone players don't have any course rights, which means, no right to pass.

Now that's more like it. Nobody around to slow me down. Nobody to bother me.

I should have guessed. But I won't let them bother me. No siree Bob. Not me.

Now that feels much better already.

OH YEEESSS! AN ACE! AN ACE! MY FIRST ACE! A HOLE IN ONE!

AN ACE! HOLE IN ONE! You saw it! You did see it didn't you!?!

Huh, what...? Sorry, I must have been busy...

Ace? I didn't see an ace? Did you see an ace?

Nope! Can't recall.

But, but...

...you were my only witnesses for my, you have to, uuuhhh, my hole... nobody will believe I hit a hole in...

...one

Later in the club house

...and I look forward once again to the tournament between Fair Haven and GCC Dolgeville!

And in keeping with tradition, all handicap classes will be allowed to compete against one another! It will definitely be an unforgettable experience for all the players and spectators...

OK, there may have been certain episodes last year such as the scorecard...

...of Dr. Jameson! But that's definitely been forgotten by now.

Please allow me to present the GCC Dolgeville tournament director, Mr. Dudek!

Thank you. How kind!

Dear golf friends, on behalf of our club I would like to express how much...

...of a privilege it is to receive you as our guest this year. Hopefully the home advantage will help us this time around, tee hee...

Here's to an exciting and fair contest...

And to make sure that we avoid the same thing as last year, I will...

...not only come along but due to the constant insistence of many players, go up against your club pro!

Who knows? Maybe it will raise our chances of winning, tee hee!

13

Hi – we have a problem – I can't talk right now but I will take care of it!

...yes I know how important this is, but I said I would take care of it! Have I ever disappointed you before? Huuhhh? what do you mean always? OK, but I promise this time will be different.

I will now present the list of players who will represent Fair Haven at this year's tournament.

Representing the ladies will be Claire Bancroft and Linda O'Connell, the men, Dr. B.T. Jameson and Charles Beidebook and the juniors, naturally Benny and Zack. We hope a large cheering section also comes along!

Seems to be my lucky day, hic, today...First a hole, hic, one and now I am on the team, hic, hooray.

Mommy what's wrong with Mr. Beidebook? He made the team but doesn't seem to be so happy...

...he seems to believe he hit a hole in one today. Just ask him for yourself!

Uumm, Mr. Beidebook, did you really hit a hole in one today? Why aren't you happy about it? I know I...

Mommmyy!
Mommmyyy!

All is silent the evening before the tournament. All are dreaming of the big win, of playing 10 under and then showing up in the club house and...oh well, we'll just have to wait 'til tomorrow.

Next stop, Dolgeville. Everybody is to meet at Fair Haven and drive in groups.

Hi boys. I would have been here sooner but I got stuck behind a Mustang only doing 120 and he wouldn't let me pass.

120? Considering the fun only begins at 140! I know exactly how you feel!

I passed 6 motorcycles on my way here without even batting an eye! What a great way to start the day! I feel sorry for the other cars on the way to Dolgeville today.

She takes off like a rocket since I had her in for some fine tuning. If you know what I mean.

I know what you mean. Give me speed or give me death! Ha ha ha. Huh?!?

Good morning gentlemen! Would it be possible to ride with one of you?

Mu husband had to deliver a baby at the last minute.

But of course! And I can promise you we will arrive long before anyone else! Ha ha.

Thanks! By the way, I'm a bit of a coward, so which one of you is a *careful* driver?

That would happen to be me! Safety is my middle name! The chariot awaits.

No, I am. People call me the snail, molasses man! That's right isn't it boys?

I had my car regulated and it doesn't drive over 40! For environmental as well as safety reasons you know.

15

This just doesn't seem like the right way Charles. Did I miss something?

I think we have to turn right up ahead. I can't believe there aren't any signs! Let me check the map.

Finally on their way...

Or is it left? Uuuhhm, you won't like this... It's not even on the map!

HICK TOWN!

A little up ahead:

Finally!

Hey buddy! Need a lift?

Just hop in the back!

Cool man!

Ha ha SUCKER! Better luck next time loser! Hee hee hee.

Shortly thereafter:

Pull over B.T. We can ask that vagrant over there! Maybe he knows.

Excuse me, you wouldn't happen to be on you way to Dolgeville would you?

Duuhhh, how'd ya guess?

16

Do you cats know the damage you do the environment with your golf courses? The flowers, the animals...

What's this world coming to man? You just don't get it!

BRRRR

You don't even care man! You think 'cause you have money you can do whatever you want. What about the flowers dude? The birds?

Now hang on a moment! You seem to be misinformed. Through the cultivation...

!

...of non-productive agricultural land, new ecological niches and natural sanctuaries are produced in the form of golf courses. These in turn serve as nesting areas for endangered birds and...

RRR

Hey Ray, ain't that the idiot we left behind? He must have a death wish!!

Are you even listening to me?

Huh? What?

Save it for the birds dude!

It's a fact, all golfers are selfish, egotistical idiots!

20

Voilà!
Dolgeville Manor!

It doesn't look very welcoming B.T.! It looks as if nobody were staying there.

I hope Errol is already here.

Don't be such a little girl! I find it homey.

I'm actually shaking! Give in, you're scared too!

Are you kidding? The only thing missing now is the hunchback butler, ha ha ha!

Good evening gentlemen. We've been expecting you.

I don't like this! Uuhh, yes, good...evening...

After you my friend!

21

You're in great form today! I thought you might still be shaking after the butler incidence...

Oh B.T., you're such a kidder. You don't actually believe that I was scared last night do...

Hhuh? **Aaaaahhh!!!**

What a nightmare!

... it's more than just a tournament!

Errol! Psst, wake up! I heard voices down stairs... Please take a look...

At the driving range:

Good morning my dear Errol, I would like to inform you of the flights if you have a moment.

The ladies will make up one flight, as well as the kids, Dr. Jameson and yourself will be playing with us in our flight.

Very sly Mr. President. Putting Errol in your flight so we can always keep our eye on him.

Not to worry, you will be happy to hear that I have made all the preparations Mr. President.

I don't either.

I don't like all that whispering.

I heard a few things last night which have made me a little skeptical.

I have the feeling that there is much more on the line here than just tournament honor.

At the same time...

Ciao my friend!

Da Presidente better'a win today since'a he like'a to bett'a so much. Peccato, if he lose'a alla da money, da golf course... And you, hunch'aback . no tricks!

26

* each course has among the official rules individual-course rules.

Wow, what a hit!

A 747!

Now that's big smoke!

And in the middle of the fairway!

ZZZZZZ

Thanks, I only hit it half face.

It looks like it's going to be a great golf day. But be careful anyway.

No problem.

The lack of trust is justified...

OK. Listen up you losers...I mean, special agents.

We are going to offer our golfers some assistance.

Huh?

I thought we were supposed to take them out because they destroy all the flowers, plants...

YOU IDIOT!!

That's fine, but just not all the golfers. Here's the plan...

Not bad Mr. President.

It was good but not good enough my dear Errol. You still won the hole.

So Pedro, I believe our opponents are going to encounter a bit of bad luck the next hole.

You're so clever Mr. President sir.

Let me check my birdie card for the next hole...

My dear Errol, don't go to all that trouble when everything is already mapped out so clearly here,...

a long par 5. Be careful here, there's a lot of water on the left side and you can't see it from the tee.

Thanks for the tip. I will make sure I stay to the right.

* One receives a penalty stroke and must drop a ball when a shot lands in the water.

And just in case there are any problems, I always have a trusty updated version of the rules with me.

That's great to know.

Very reassuring.

The player with the lowest handicap has the honor – Moi!

I'm playing a white Competition ultra 5-xcl. with red lettering.

What's the compression...?

Seems to have drifted out of bounds.

You can play another ball temporarily.

Don't worry, *I'll find it!*

A while later...

I don't want to rush you but the 5 minutes are up!

And remember, we're playing strictly by the Dolgeville golf rules.

A little exercise that is...

Anyway, you know what I mean.

I don't know what I would do without my trainer Jeff – I sweat a gallon during his step-aerobic classes.

Speaking of sweating, this heat definitely doesn't do my expensive designer clothing any good.

What a pity...

I can imagine it being extremely hard for you.

What is?

Well, I mean with your weight and all.

Thanks, I'm just fine with it.

And to top it off, you have to pull this heavy golf bag as well...

Nobody pulls or carries their own bag any more.

And don't even bother to tell me how healthy, sporty and all that jiberish it is. I don't carry mine and look at me...

See this remote control? It gives off a signal and my Electro-Caddy is never far behind. Following my every move.

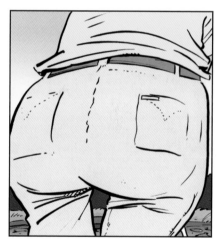

And finally, the 18th hole:

We're tied. The excitement mounts.

It would be more prudent to play the ball in front of the water rather than risking going for the green.

I hope you understood that! Play cautiously do you hear!

Psst, come on now "pro" – you can make the green with your eyes shut.

Ya, right... n..no problem!

!

"There he is – the star we've all been waiting for."

"His first year on the tour and he's only moments away from sealing the victory and the masters."

"Pedro "Tiger" Ramirez: The man who can add a page to the history books today..."

The spectators and the millions of viewers at home are definitely excited about his next move. Ramirez looks quite relaxed...This is the shot which will decide it all... What will he do?

quiet

"And he goes for the green!!"

41

...And in rare cases, some even get carried away.

SCORE 78

OK gentlemen, let's have all the cards on the table so we can count the individual scores.

Don't let it get you down Daddy, I didn't hit well today either!

Check it out, the shrimp inherited his dad's talent, ha ha ha!

Is that so...?

On that weed field, no wonder!

Are you saying it's the course's fault?

43

45